BACKTALK

BACKTALK

Press Councils in America

By William L. Rivers, Stanford University
William B. Blankenburg, University of Wisconsin
Kenneth Starck, University of South Carolina
Earl Reeves, University of Tulsa

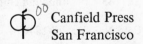 Canfield Press
San Francisco

A Department of Harper & Row, Publishers, Inc.
New York, Evanston, London

Dedicated to the Memory of
Lowell Mellett

Contents

Introduction

by BEN H. BAGDIKIAN

Assistant Managing Editor and Ombudsman, The Washington *Post*
President, The Mellett Fund for a Free and Responsible Press

How can a small foundation accomplish something useful about press performance in this country—with only $40,000?

This was pretty much the charter presented the trustees of the Mellett Fund for a Free and Responsible Press in 1966. One outcome is this book. We decided to support university researchers in establishing local press councils and publish the results, hoping this would produce beneficial results for the press and its public.

The idea of press councils is not new. Britain has a national Press Council which was first proposed by the Royal Commission on the Press in 1943. The Council consists of nonjournalists who monitor the English press, issue an annual audit on performance, and require offenders to print corrections. A national council with somewhat the same duties was recommended for the United States in 1947 by the (Hutchins) Commission on Freedom of the Press, but never materialized. In 1963, Barry Bingham, president and editor of the Louisville *Courier-Journal* and *Times*, suggested the establishment of *local* press councils as a forum between a paper and its community. The idea was tried spasmodically, usually by individual publishers or editors, but never with detailed dissemination of results. Even so, where it was tried, publishers claimed that they learned much about the community and the community much about newspapers.

The local press council appealed to the Mellett Fund for a number of reasons. First, it seemed eminently suited to typical American papers, which are local, whereas a national council would have to look at 1750 papers or a large sample of them. Second, it had never before been tried as independent projects carefully designed and recorded to produce a body of experience available to the whole trade.

Third, a small number of projects could have a multiplied effect if results caused other publishers and other committees to make spontaneous efforts of their own. And fourth, we hoped we could afford it.

We decided on a number of ground rules:

1. The local council would have no power, and no impression of power, to force change in the local paper. It could study, discuss, or vote, always with the publisher as a member of the group. But the paper retained discretion over its own contents.

2. The local council would not be organized by the paper. Any proposal would have the cooperation of the paper, of course, but the researcher would select council members. And members would understand that they had no power over editing the paper but were still gathered as equals with the publisher in council proceedings.

3. The design, implementation, and reporting of the council experience would be by a university researcher. Once we were satisfied of his qualifications and his plan we exercised no control over his experiment or his report at the end of the year.

4. A major objective of the enterprise was to be a detailed analysis of the experience of the researcher, the results to be given the widest possible dissemination.

Having each project totally controlled by a university researcher had many advantages: He would have the training and discipline to design and operate a valid experiment. He would know the papers and the communities in his area but would be minimally beholden to any parties on the council. He would ensure that the local councils were independent of any vested interest in the newspaper field.

Leaving the design to the researcher, the Fund asked those making proposals to consider such issues as: how often a press council would meet to permit continuity and detailed discussion but to avoid excessive burdens on busy people; how large the council should be and how a valid community representation would be made; whether the publisher alone would represent the paper or whether staff members whose work was under question would attend; whether council members alone could attend and speak at meetings, or whether interested members of the public could come at will; whether the council would be solely a discussion group or whether it would take formal votes on questions of fairness, accuracy, and responsibility; and whether council proceedings would be given maximum or minimum publicity at the time of their meetings. The Fund also asked universities to suggest different rules for various projects if they found them feasible in order to learn which produced the best results.

The response was encouraging. Some university journalism departments with reputations for rigorous and imaginative research submitted proposals. The response for a number of publishers was similarly productive—some, for example, volunteered the names of their most bitter critics for possible inclusion in the local council.

The Mellett Fund is named in honor of Lowell Mellett, the first editor of the Washington *Daily News*, a post he held for sixteen years. Following World War II, during which he was adviser to President Roosevelt, he returned to newspapering as a syndicated columnist. When he died in 1960, he left the American Newspaper Guild, of which he had been a member, 1884 shares of Scripps-Howard Investment Co., a nonoperating entity that holds stock in individual Scripps-Howard papers but has no controlling interest in any of them and exercises no function in labor-management relations. His bequest directed that the money be used to encourage more responsible performance by the press without infringing First Amendment freedoms. He specifically hoped, in fact, that his bequest could help establish "a relationship between the people and the press whereby full responsibility for its behavior would be met by the press."

It was some years before final settlement of the Mellett estate and before organization of the Mellett Fund. Upon receipt of the shares (which constitute less than one-half of 1 percent of Scripps-Howard Investment), the Guild sold them to its Defense Fund at the court-established value and turned the proceeds over to the Mellett account. As a result of this sale, the Fund's assets are entirely in cash.

The Mellett Fund was incorporated as a nonprofit corporation in Washington, D.C. Initially it had a paid coordinator to compile information on possible projects and to arrange proper incorporation. It now has no regular employees and all trustees serve without pay. The first president was Alan Barth, editorialist for the Washington *Post*. When he had to resign because of demands of other duties, I (originally vice-president) was elected president.

The Fund has had encouragement and cooperation from the largest single source of research, the Association for Education in Journalism. At an annual meeting, the AEJ commended the Fund for helping create a mechanism that "could contribute significantly to improvements in the quality of mass communication in the U.S."

BACKTALK

CHAPTER ONE

The Dinosaur and His Critics

by WILLIAM L. RIVERS

> There is a story, perhaps apocryphal, that the dinosaur did not go out of existence because he was too big or clumsy. What really happened was that he suffered a failure of communication. His brain did not transmit signals to his foot—and his foot back to his brain—rapidly and accurately enough to create a picture of reality on which the dinosaur could act.
>
> —Douglass Cater,
> author and press critic

In a few cities across the United States, groups of laymen meet regularly with newspapermen and broadcasters to discuss the problems of their communities and to assess the way the news media report and interpret them. These press councils, as most of them are called—they are also variously known as "mass media councils," "community-media councils," and "communications councils"—are new kinds of channels between the mass media and the people. Although they have no real power and can do no more than advise and criticize, these councils may be the vanguard of a movement that will change the nature of journalism in the United States. For this may be remembered as the time when Americans made the performance of the mass media the people's business.

What these groups can accomplish is suggested by a recent action of the Honolulu Community-Media Council. One member, John Witeck, complained at the April 1971 meeting that the news media mislead by reporting the conflict in Indochina in such objectionable terms as *Vietcong, enemy, Communist forces, Reds, Communist China*, and *Red China*. He suggested that more acceptable terms would be those used by the organizations themselves: *National Liberation Front*

(NLF), *Provisional Revolutionary Government* (PRG), *Democratic Republic of Vietnam, North Vietnamese, People's Republic of China, China, Mainland China, National United Front* (in Cambodia), and *Pathet Lao* (in Laos).

A council "committee on euphemisms" monitored three television stations, two radio stations, two daily newspapers, and two wire services for ten days in May. Among the findings were the fact that UPI used "communist" 121 times and "North Vietnamese" only seventeen times. Such reporting "creates and maintains certain negative images in the minds of the reading and listening public," the committee reported. The members recommended that the media avoid "umbrella or catch-all terms which do not accurately and in detail describe the people to which they refer, except where warranted and fully explained." The report continued:

> We are particularly concerned with the use of such terms as "communist" and "enemy" which are too easily employed to refer to a wide variety of people and organizations in Indochina. These terms should be avoided as much as possible in favor of more descriptive terms which accurately designate the people or organizations to which they refer. In this regard we recommend the following questions as guidelines:
>
> a. When opposing forces meet, who actually make up the opposing forces? What organizations are involved? Does the word "communist" accurately describe who they are? Can everyone who is fighting against the South Vietnamese government be described as a "communist"?
>
> b. When death tolls are announced, who actually has been killed? Are they military personnel, or are they civilians? Can everyone who is killed be accurately described as an "enemy"? Is a person an "enemy" simply because he has been killed by the South Vietnamese? . . .
>
> . . . In order to bring about greater accuracy in local news reporting on the Indochina conflict, we recommend that local subscribers to wire services and syndicated and network materials (i.e., TV, radio, newspapers) institute a policy of asking for greater accuracy in detailed reporting from the sources of news coverage. . . .

The committee report was adopted unanimously. It was as though the council agreed with Confucius that the most important concern of any society is that language be correct. ("If language is not correct, then what is said is not what is meant; if what is said is not meant, then what ought to be done remains undone; if this remains undone, then morals and art deteriorate; if morals and art deteriorate, justice will go astray; if justice goes astray, the people will stand about in helpless confusion. Hence there must be no arbitrariness in what is said. This matters above everything.")

Moreover, Roger Tatarian, vice-president and editor of UPI, cited the Honolulu council's resolution approvingly in a newsletter circulated among UPI employees and clients. The council had been careful to point up the frequent difficulties in ascertaining identities in Vietnam, and Tatarian emphasized these points. But his letter ended: "We certainly agree with the Honolulu Community-Media Council that specifics are preferable to generalities and should be used wherever possible." After that, UPI reporters and editors are not likely to use "communist" carelessly. The effect may be profound. UPI has thousands of newspaper and broadcast clients in the United States and thousands of others over the rest of the world.

Such successes are, of course, isolated incidents. Whether press councils will become a significant force will not be known for several years. The movement is still small and its shape is indistinct. It is difficult even to describe press councils precisely because they appear in so many forms. In some cities, they are blue-ribbon groups made up of involved and articulate citizens. Elsewhere, the membership is an occupational cross section or a mixture of a cross section and a blue-ribbon group. Although most councils discuss everything about the media from the trivial to the cosmic, a few have a narrower focus, notably those that bring blacks and whiles together to argue, often explosively, the reporting of minority interests. Some councils continue for years. Others have lasted for only a few months, dying

Dr. Rivers, Professor of Communication at Stanford University, is author of The Opinionmakers, The Adversaries, *and other books. He writes a column, "Monitoring Media," for* The Progressive.

because the mission was accomplished in some cases—and because it could not be accomplished. Most councils are small in size and located in small cities. But the Honolulu council has thirty-one members, and the city has a population of more than 300,000. In Minnesota, the daily newspapers have created a statewide council.

In all this wild variety, the only common feature is a striking one: newspapermen and broadcasters are meeting regularly and willingly with their critics. The editor of the Honolulu *Advertiser*, George Chaplin, emphasized the importance of this fact. When I asked him during a meeting of the Honolulu council how the editors and publishers of thirty years ago would have reacted to press councils, he replied, "They'd have said that what they did was none of the public's damned business." No doubt Chaplin is right. The great majority of press executives of earlier days probably agreed with William Peter Hamilton of the *Wall Street Journal:* "A newspaper is a private enterprise owing nothing whatever to the public, which grants it no franchise. It is therefore affected with no public interest. It is emphatically the property of the owner, who is selling a manufactured product at his own risk...."[1] *Editor & Publisher*, the trade weekly of the newspaper industry, is undoubtedly right in saying that today most editors and publishers will cooperate with any council that is established.[2] *TV Guide* argued that broadcasters should work to establish a national media council.[3]

What is behind this change?

The Many Loud Critics

Part of the answer is that the media are reacting to a flood of criticism. As Newbold Noyes of the Washington *Star* said in 1970, on becoming president of the American Society of Newspaper Editors, "The American press and the concept of press freedom is under more serious attack today than at any time in this century." And as NBC News director Reuven Frank has written, the intellectual and middle-brow critics of television are now being joined by "the basic American audience, the most middle-class majority in history."

The trend began to emerge in 1964 at the Republican National Convention when the delegates roared their approval as former President Dwight Eisenhower damned the "columnists and commentators." The pattern was even clearer at the 1968 Democratic National Convention: while, on the one hand, the radicals on the streets of Chicago attacked the media as capitalist tools, on the other hand, conservatives watching television—until then the most trusted news medium because "pictures don't lie"—refused to believe what the television pictures were showing them of police brutality against the young radicals, choosing instead to believe that the police were responding to provocation deliberately obscured by the liberal TV reporters.

By 1970, suspicion of the mass media was spread across the political spectrum from right to left. In one incident, Vice President Spiro Agnew, by then famous for diatribes against the news media, was scheduled to speak at a Northern California conference on "The Mass Media, Public Opinion, and Foreign Policy." It was expected, of course, that in his speech he would attack again, but the Cambodian invasion forced him to cancel his appearance. Ironically, some of his antagonists attacked for him: a dozen young radicals interrupted the conference with splashy signs that charged: "The Media Lie!"

Now right and left argue that American journalism distorts and lies for the other. Though once journalists took comfort in simply damning this as irrationality, in fact the news media *are* at both ends of the spectrum. Most publishers and broadcast executives are Republicans—few so reactionary as to wish the restoration of William McKinley, but most conservative enough to uphold the status quo and convince the radical leftists that they are united in a conspiracy to create docile consumers. Likewise, Agnew and other conservative Republicans have good reasons to suspect working journalists, for most reporters *are* liberals, as Agnew has charged. And if they are not quite radical leftists, they speak enough of the language to seem dangerous.

Actually, the biases of right-leaning proprietors and left-leaning journalists may cancel each other. But in troubled times, both the right and the left find comfort in believing the media are slanted against them. And the fact that this is indeed a troubled period partly explains the passion of the critics; it is traditional to attack the messenger who brings the bad news.

But even attacking the messenger has a kind of logic. For the modern messengers do not bring a single item of news; they select among a thousand items every day, deciding which to play up and which to ignore. It is not surprising, therefore, that they are excoriated by some for emphasizing today's grim problems and by others for not coming to grips with these same problems. However their messages are delivered—in one sentence, ten, or a hundred—even if there is no distortion at the sending end of the channel, human communication is so liable to error that there is likely to be distortion at the receiving end. One need not even consider intentions; accidental distortions generate enough rancor.

The central question as the 1970s began was whether attacks on the news media would increase—perhaps even increase to the point where violence would continually mar the relationship between the press and its audience. There were, in fact, many violent episodes. Cameramen trying to record the concession statement of Hugh Addonizio, who had failed in his reelection attempt to be mayor of Newark, New Jersey, were pushed and buffeted by Addonizio supporters who blamed television for his defeat. A San Francisco *Chronicle* reporter was savagely beaten at a school board meeting. The editor of the Bellevue, Nebraska, *Press* experienced having his car fire-bombed. A Houston radio station found its $30,000 transmitter dynamited.

The Problem of "Distance"

Somewhat ironically, news executives are also recognizing that they must reduce the distance that stretches between the media and the public. At one time, many newspapers (and magazines) served many publics. If each paper had a relatively slender circulation, the editor nevertheless spoke directly to the central interests of his readers and could usually count on their loyalty. His views might be opposed, and his plant might be attacked (many abolitionist papers were destroyed), but most readers opposed to the editor's views subscribed to papers that squared with their own prejudices.

As newspapers and magazines became larger and fewer, and editors became obliged to corral mass audiences, separate voices could no longer easily be raised in the hitherto "free marketplace of ideas." As the astute observer of journalism Wilbur Schramm has commented: "The small, numerous media, as we knew them in the Eighteenth and Nineteenth Centuries, were representative of the people . . . in fact, they *were* the people. But the larger and more centralized media have to some extent withdrawn from the people and become a separate set of institutions, parallel and comparable with other power centers such as business and government."

The only business specifically protected by the Constitution, the press was given its broad measure of freedom precisely so that citizens could have the information needed to participate fully in democracy. "A people who mean to be their own governors," James Madison wrote, "will arm themselves with the power knowledge gives. A popular government without popular information is but a prologue to a farce, or a tragedy, or perhaps both." But as government became larger and more distant, the press became much more a business, and almost equally distant. At the turn of the twentieth century, Lincoln Steffens, a keen analyst of American institutions, reported that newspaper executives, talking shop at a convention, had spoken of their properties as factories and likened editorial management to that of department stores. "Journalism today is a business," Steffens wrote, with a little of the awe of discovery.

Later critics—Will Irwin, Upton Sinclair, George Seldes—made clear exactly how businesslike many newspapers had become. Writer A. J. Liebling described the press thus: "It is the weak slat under the bed of democracy. It is an anomaly that information, the one thing most necessary to our survival as choosers of our own way, should be a commodity subject to the same rules as chewing gum, while armament, a secondary instrument of liberty, is a government concern. A man is not free if he cannot see where he is going, even if he has a gun to help him get there."

Some editors and broadcasters began to realize years ago that the distance between journalist and reader had become too vast for effective two-way communication. A few editors enlarged their letters-to-the-editor space and started "Action Line" columns to encourage readers to bring their thoughts to the newspaper. Some radio and television stations began to program call-in and talk shows to give listeners and viewers a chance to speak.

But many critics view these as only token measures to forestall criticism. Indeed, some suspect not just this newspaper or that editor, this station or that newscaster, but *all* the "media" (how quickly the word has become a familiar label).

Those arguing minority causes are especially apt to emphasize their lack of access to the media. Professor Jerome Barron of George Washington University supports this viewpoint when he argues that the free press guarantee of the First Amendment was meant to assure that every voice should be heard, but actually only the media proprietors have been given real freedom—and because proprietors have prevented some voices from being heard by denying them access to the only channels to our massive, complex society, the First Amendment must be reinterpreted to provide full access.[4]

In 1969, two years after Barron wrote this, broadcasters argued before the U.S. Supreme Court that the First Amendment protected their right to put on the air whatever they chose and to exclude from the air whomever they chose. The Court held, however, that:

> . . . as far as the First Amendment is concerned those who are licensed stand no better than those to whom licenses are refused. A license permits broadcasting, but the licensee has no constitutional right to be the one who holds the license or to monopolize a radio frequency to the exclusion of his fellow citizens. There is nothing in the First Amendment which prevents the government from requiring a licensee to share his frequency with others and to . . . present those views and voices which are representative of his community and which would otherwise, by necessity, be barred from the airwaves.[5]

The decision does not affect print media and requires only that broadcasters allow responses to views that have been broadcast; nevertheless, it is at least a step toward a "new" First Amendment. So far, the rule has proved workable, largely because broadcasting devotes so little time anyway to presenting controversial views that it is no strain to provide time for response. But similar rules would be difficult for newspapers. Clifton Daniel, associate editor of the New York *Times*, pointed out that in one recent year the *Times* received 37,719 letters to the editor—and that if all eighteen million words in those letters had been printed (and every letter-writer probably thought he had a right of access), they would have filled 135 complete issues of the paper. Nonetheless, the freedom of the print media to use their columns as they wish is a deep source of bitterness among many readers.

The Insider's Criticism

Perhaps the chief reason news executives are no longer so belligerently defensive is that some of their employees are among the most vehement critics. At one time, reporters who were themselves privately critical reacted to outside attacks like a herd of angry animals, rumps together, horns out. Some still react that way. But few outsiders can match the acid insights of the journalist critics, which are now quite public. Almost any news medium of size and pretensions to excellence harbors fierce critics and perhaps an incipient revolt among its younger, brighter reporters. This is much more than the traditional grousing of the tyro who thinks that the old-timers are naturally old-fashioned. It means that those older journalists who believe that their present efforts are sufficient unto the need of the hour don't know what time it is. Ben Bagdikian, one of the older men who sympathize with most of the aspirations of the young reporters, has written: "Trying to be a first-rate reporter on the average American newspaper is like trying to play Bach's St. Matthew's Passion on a ukelele: the instrument is too crude for the work, for the audience, and for the performer." This wraps up in a sentence a major fault of American journalism, which is so devoted to the isolated fact that it ignores the necessity for interpreting: for clarifying, explaining, and placing facts in a meaningful context.

The need for interpreting is a persistent theme in many of the reviews of the performance of their own papers that journalists are publishing in New York, Chicago, Honolulu, St. Louis, Denver, Philadelphia, Providence, and other cities. The stories in these reviews cover the full range of irresponsible actions by newspapers and broadcasting stations, but it is remarkable how many cases spring from the fact that management favors its friends. Working journalists are especially scornful of country-club journalism.

There is also scorn for the timid kind of editing that suppresses facts. A review published by Associated Press staffers recounted how AP editors butchered a report from Cambodia by Peter Arnett, a Pulitzer-Prize-winning correspondent. Arnett related that "American tanks captured the Cambodian plantation town of Snoul Wednesday morning after U.S. air strikes destroyed 90 per cent of it. The American soldiers celebrated the victory by tearing down the Cambodian flag over the district capital and looting the few shops undamaged." His dispatch described the looting and reported that when an officer ordered the men to "Get your hands off that stuff," they laughed and loaded the booty in their vehicles.

But when the report reached U.S. newspapers, all references to looting had been deleted by the editors in New York. The AP foreign editor cabled the AP office in Saigon:

> WE ARE IN THE MIDST OF A HIGHLY CHARGED SITUATION IN
> UNISTATES REGARDING SOUTHEAST ASIA AND MUST GUARD
> OUR COPY TO SEE THAT IT IS DOWN THE MIDDLE AND SUBDUES
> EMOTION. SPECIFICALLY TODAY WE TOOK LOOTING AND SIMI-
> LAR REFERENCES OUT OF ARNETT COPY BECAUSE WE DON'T
> THINK IT'S ESPECIALLY NEWS THAT SUCH THINGS TAKE PLACE
> IN WAR AND IN PRESENT CONTEXT THIS CAN BE INFLAMMA-
> TORY.

The cable explained similar deletions in another story and ended:

> LET'S PLAY IT COOL.

The foreign editor did not include in his cable what he had told
the deskmen who had edited Arnett's story: "We can't let the Agnews
seize upon this sort of thing."

Even broadcast journalists, who traditionally keep most of their
complaints to themselves, are beginning to grumble out loud. Some
contribute to the published journalism reviews. (In St. Louis, the staff
members of a noncommercial radio station, KDNA-FM, have developed
an instant journalism review by criticizing television news shows while
they are being broadcast. The listener-viewer puts a television newscast
on his screen, then turns the volume down on the TV set and up on a
radio tuned to KDNA. Four experts criticize the telecast as it is being
shown.) Young staffers at New York's WPIX-TV and at San Francisco's
KRON-TV have charged before the Federal Communications Commission that management caused falsifications of the news. Many protest
the very basis of television news: the primacy of show business over
reporting, which causes television to feature the visual and the dramatic
to the point of distortion. Journalist Henry Fairlie points out that the
problems begin with the time limitations on televised reports and with
television's tendency to produce self-generating news—that is, the presence of TV cameras themselves may, for example, incite acts of violence during abrasive situations. Fairlie also points to the misleading
effects caused by the size of the screen. For instance, during one report,
television showed some

> . . . alarming pictures of white men and women in the Chicago
> suburb of Cicero screaming abuse at some Negro marchers. Their
> hating faces—a dozen of them, perhaps—filled the screen. They

looked as if they were a representative sample of a much larger crowd. But anyone who was there knows that these particular whites were only a small part of the crowds in the streets; and that the crowds themselves were only a small part of the total white population of Cicero. To this vital extent, television that night distorted badly.[6]

The vehemence and the sincerity of those journalists who work for change, plus outside pressures, have caused some news executives to question traditional practices. Seldom do they cry "freedom of the press" when journalistic rights are challenged these days; instead they appeal to "the public's right to know"—implicitly recognizing that their freedom exists for a purpose and that it must be justified. One of the most striking evidences that criticism has provoked thought among executives came when Newbold Noyes, editor of the Washington *Star* and President of the American Society of Newspaper Editors (ASNE), spoke at the annual meeting of the ASNE in 1971. His speech was a catalogue of journalistic failings that made Noyes, a middle-aged conservative, sound like a young liberal reporter. He called the news formulas used by his and other papers "simplistic" and "childish." He said that newspapers must grow up and change because readers are entitled to more than they are getting. He added:

> Why is a speech, a press conference, a court decision, a congressional hearing always news, while the real situations behind these surface things go unnoted? Why? Because it is easy that way, and because that is the way we have always done it. Editors and publishers may fault the deskman who overlooks a handout—but who will miss it if he fails to ask the question that illuminates the cause of the handout? We do not even bother to cover the surface events in any but the most superficial way. Look at what we do with speeches, for instance—have you ever seen a news story which really reflected the content and intent of a speech? The reporter, doing as we have taught him, looks for one startling or contentious or silly statement, and there is his lead. He backs it up with one or two direct or indirect quotes, adds a couple of paragraphs as background, and there's your story. . . .
>
> Look at our basic concepts of news. Not only do we devote 80

percent of our time and space to the sorts of stereotyped happenings I have mentioned, but we also insist that these happenings are newsworthy only if they meet certain stereotyped standards. There is no story in a speech or a press conference or what-have-you unless it involves conflict or surprise.

Before a situation is worthy of our attention, it must burst to the surface in some disruptive, exceptional (and hence newsworthy) event. Even when we know what is happening under the surface, we are forever waiting for a traditional news peg to hang the story on. What are we thinking of, sticking to such old-fashioned concepts in a time of revolutionary movement? If we have so little faith in the intelligence of our readers, how can we expect them to have faith in us? No wonder the readers constantly feel that events are overwhelming them, unawares.[7]

The Climate for Councils

Despite all the soul-searching and admissions of incompetence and guilt, few news executives are eager to embrace press councils. *Editor & Publisher* is probably right in holding that most will cooperate with councils established by others but they are not likely to form the councils themselves. This reluctance lingers from the years of independence the press has enjoyed. The reluctance of some newsmen also springs from what they have heard about European councils—and about the oppressive statutory councils in less-developed countries. Since Sweden formed the Press Fair Practices Commission in 1916 as an intermediary between press and public, about fifteen other European nations have established similar bodies, with the British Press Council being the most famous and successful. Generally, European councils protect press freedom, channel helpful dialogues between newspapers and readers, and advise and publicize without having statutory strength. In a few European countries, however—notably Spain and Portugal—the press does not have the freedom it enjoys in the United States, and councils sometimes exert a coercive power.

In the United States, however, the entire history of press councils grows out of an atmosphere of freedom. The idea of American press councils was probably first conceived in the 1930s by Chilton Bush, then head of the Stanford Department of Communication, who believed that newspapers could strengthen themselves and their communities by working with groups of citizens who would regularly offer criticisms and suggestions. Bush promoted the idea among California publishers, at first in vain. In 1950, William Townes, publisher of the Santa Rosa *Press Democrat,* decided to try it.

Townes chose the members of his "citizens' advisory council" to represent community interests—labor, education, agriculture, city government, and business—and included a few outspoken critics of his policies. At the first meeting, Townes told council members that although he alone would decide publishing policies, he would welcome criticisms and suggestions. That meeting began hesitantly, but at subsequent meetings the members engaged in lively discussions. Townes spent most of his time listening. He did not even have to defend his paper against its harshest critic, a judge specifically asked to serve on the council because he was a well-known opponent of the *Press Democrat*; the other members were quick to challenge unfounded criticisms. Townes kept the council operating until he left Santa Rosa in 1951 and said that it helped him improve his paper. As *Editor & Publisher* commented:

> On the practical side, this particular newspaper reports that council meetings revealed several important stories that had not been covered. And council members felt free to visit the newspaper offices thereafter, something many of them might not have thought about previously.
>
> This is an experiment in getting closer to the community which strikes us as valuable. The good points outweigh the bad, and if conducted properly and regularly can only result to the benefit of the paper.[8]

Despite this endorsement, the press council idea languished for years. To be sure, Barry Bingham, president and editor of the two Louisville, Kentucky, papers, the *Courier-Journal* and the *Times*, publicly urged that local press councils be established and for his own papers appointed an ombudsman to investigate readers' complaints. And local councils were tried here and there in the '50s and '60s, a typical effort being that of California publisher Ray Spangler, who regularly asked a few community leaders for advice on how his Redwood City *Tribune* could deal with the city's problems. But it was not until 1967 that the press council began to take on its present dimensions.

In that year Ben Bagdikian became president of the Mellett Fund for a Free and Responsible Press. This small foundation had only $40,000 with which to carry out Lowell Mellett's wish that his bequest be used to encourage responsible press performance without infringing First Amendment freedoms. Bagdikian suggested that the money be used to support university researchers in making press council experiments. The result was that six councils were established. Four of them were newspaper councils (one in California, one in Oregon, and two in Illinois). Another council was established in Seattle and still another in St. Louis, involving broadcasters as well as publishers. The Seattle and St. Louis councils brought the newsmen together with spokesmen for the black community in each city.

There was little coordination or correspondence among those who established the first councils. As the case studies that make up much of the rest of this book suggest, the researchers adhered to the broad rules laid down by the Mellett Fund, but they set up, operated, and evaluated their councils in different ways. Despite the absence of coordination and the differences in size among the cities involved (from Sparta, Illinois, with its population of 3500, to St. Louis, Missouri, with 750,000)—not to mention the differences in focus and purpose between the general press councils and those devoted to the problems of blacks—there were remarkable similarities. For at one time or another, most of the councils dealt with most of the central issues of mass communication in modern society.

For example, a continuing question in journalism is the stance of the editor or broadcaster. He may be "community oriented" and seek consensus, perhaps even to the point of glossing over faults to promote what he considers to be the greater good. His editorials are likely to be innocuous—or even nonexistent. Or he may be "journalist oriented" and stress conflict, printing or broadcasting all the facts he can discover even though they may present to the community a view of itself that many citizens would prefer to ignore. At least a few of his editorials will injure some readers. The typology is not really so neat, of course. The "journalist," however dedicated to disclosure, almost automatically publishes much that promotes the community's betterment and image in a way that the Chamber of Commerce approves. And the "community" man will at least on occasion print or broadcast news and editorials that reveal flaws. It may be, too, that the majority of newspapermen and broadcasters shift between "community" and "journalist" orientations depending upon the issue, the personalities involved, and the circumstances.

The press councils met this basic question from a number of perspectives. They discussed community leadership. Is leading a basic function of the press? Should a newspaper crusade? They discussed public relations. Should the press be the PR organ of the community? They discussed culture. Should the press promote the arts?

The councils also grappled with a question that thoughtful journalists have been debating for years: Does the grant of freedom carry with it a demand that the press be responsible? If so, who is to decide responsible performance?

Questions that have sprung from recent events were also central to the discussions: Does the press make news in the process of covering it? Should the problems of minorities get special attention?

Because these discussions were practical rather than theoretical—in terms of events in St. Louis and Sparta and Redwood City—and because they involved many laymen who had never considered such problems, there is a freshness of approach and idea that adds significantly to the long dialogue.

The rest of this book explores five council experiences in chapters written by the researchers.[9] Chapters 2 and 3 were written by Dr. William B. Blankenburg, associate professor of journalism at the University of Wisconsin, who worked with me in establishing and operating nine-member councils in Redwood City, California, and Bend, Oregon. The California council was a cross section of the community, with members chosen by occupation. The Oregon Council was made up of leaders of Bend and its area (although the membership was chosen with some regard for differences in sex and occupation, with known critics of the paper being sought).

The sessions in both Redwood City and Bend were monthly dinner meetings lasting three to four hours. Redwood City *Tribune* publisher Ray Spangler and editor David Schutz attended regularly. *Bulletin* editor-owner Robert Chandler met regularly with the Bend council. On two occasions, *Bulletin* managing editor William Yates attended, and *Bulletin* reporter Dan Perry attended one meeting.

Chapters 4 and 5 were written by Dr. Kenneth Starck, associate professor of journalism at the University of South Carolina (who at the time of the council experiments taught at Southern Illinois University). In Sparta, Illinois, Dr. Starck chose sixteen members to represent a cross section of the community. Twelve were active throughout. William Morgan, publisher of the Sparta *News-Plaindealer*, attended the monthly meetings regularly. The council decided—and Morgan agreed—

that because Morgan was on a first-name basis with most of the members and his presence might inhibit criticism, he should attend only the second half of each meeting.

In Cairo, Illinois, Dr. Starck had trouble establishing the council. Two black leaders—the president of the local NAACP and an official of the Council for Illinois Migrant Workers—could not be invited to serve because of the objections of nearly every white prospect and several of the other blacks. Of the fifteen Cairo residents who agreed to serve on the council, ten participated actively throughout the experience. Martin Brown, who was then editor and general manager of the Cairo *Evening Citizen*, attended regularly except for the first three meetings, which were devoted to discussing the major theories underlying press functions and responsibilities.

Dr. Earl Reeves, who wrote Chapters 6 and 7, is director of Special Undergraduate Programs in Urban Fields at the University of Tulsa. Dr. Reeves established the Community Communications Council of St. Louis when he taught at the University of Missouri—St. Louis. He invited representatives of all the major news media of the city to participate. Concerned that the black membership on the council should be broadly representative, Dr. Reeves asked black individuals and organizations to list those who should be invited to serve. The lists were combined (there was substantial overlap), and the number pared to twelve. Later, two other blacks were added.

To understand the fears of news executives in 1967, when the first two of the press councils described in this book were set up, it is instructive to know what happened when it was announced that Robert W. Chandler, editor-owner of the Bend *Bulletin*, and Ray Spangler, publisher of the Redwood City *Tribune*, had agreed to work with local councils. Each received an unnerving letter from a high executive of the *Wall Street Journal*. The letter asked: "Why are you giving up your press freedom?"

Notes

[1] Quoted in Fred S. Siebert *et al.*, *Four Theories of the Press* (Urbana, Ill.: University of Illinois Press, 1969), p. 73.

[2] "What About Press Councils?" *Editor & Publisher*, November 28, 1970, p. 4.

[3] *TV Guide*, May 30, 1970, p. 1.

[4] Jerome Barron, "Access to the Press—A New First Amendment Right," *Harvard Law Review*, 1967.

[5] Quoted in William L. Rivers *et al., The Mass Media and Modern Society* (San Francisco: Rinehart Press, 1971), pp. 6-7.

[6] Henry Fairlie, "Can You Believe Your Eyes?", *Horizon*, Spring 1967, p. 25.

[7] Newbold Noyes, "Ethics: What ASNE Is All About," *Nieman Reports*, June 1971, p. 15.

[8] "Advisory Council," *Editor & Publisher*, July 28, 1951, p. 36.

[9] Dr. Lawrence Schneider, associate professor of journalism at San Fernando Valley State College, conducted a press council experiment in Seattle with Mellett Fund support when he taught at the University of Washington. He elected to report on that experience independently rather than contribute to this volume. He has written an excellent article, "A Media-Black Council: Seattle's 19-Month Experiment," that appeared in the Autumn 1970 issue of *Journalism Quarterly*, and he expects to include more on the Seattle council in a forthcoming book on urban journalism.

CHAPTER TWO

Press Councils and Press Freedom

by WILLIAM B. BLANKENBURG

> A press council establishes a communica-
> tions link with the public—valid to the ex-
> tent that the council is a cross section of the
> community—which could well feed new
> ideas into tired newspaper minds.
>
> —Ray Spangler, publisher,
> Redwood City *Tribune*

On a crisp February morning in Redwood City, California, a slim eighteen-year-old named Jim Feyler arose and contemplated his first day as a newsboy. Feyler had held a number of odd jobs, but this was his first venture into the nation's only Constitutionally protected industry, the newspaper business. He eluded the Horatio Alger image. His hair was lank, red dustmop, and a gauzy little beard curled from his chin. He didn't care if you called him a hippie.

Just before noon he ambled along Redwood City's El Camino Real and began a soft sell of an armload of two underground papers, the *San Francisco Banner Herald* and the *Southern California Oracle.* Neither newspaper will ever win a Pulitzer Prize, but like many such journals they are highly regarded by the people they serve. Sequoia High School students were Feyler's best customers, and he sold thirty papers in his first three hours.

An alert reporter for the Redwood City *Tribune* interviewed Feyler, and the next day the *Tribune* informed its 21,000 subscribers that a "psychedelic newsboy" was in their midst. "I'll be here every working day from noon to sunset or until I sell out," the *Tribune* story quoted Feyler, next to a photograph showing him smiling wanly.

Redwood City doesn't seem to be a town that would worry about a scruffy youth on its streets. A suburban city of 65,000 located twenty-five miles south of San Francisco, it is hardly backwoods, even though it began as a lumber camp. It is now an international port and an industrial center. In 1968, according to its chamber of commerce, Redwood City was "A Centennial City in Action." But the day after the *Tribune* story, Deputy Chief of Police Ted Moudakas announced that his office was "bombarded" with irate calls from citizens who wanted Feyler run out of town. One woman threatened to take vigilante action.

Moudakas was not unhappy with the response. "With support like this," he said, "police work is much easier." Adding that he didn't intend to deprive anyone of his rights, Moudakas nevertheless exhumed a thirty-year-old ordinance forbidding merchandising on city streets without a license and sent Officer Donald E. Wilkes to tell Feyler that he needed a $10 permit. Wilkes reported back: "He departed a little unhappy but said he would comply with our wishes." Feyler never did apply for a permit, nor did he return.

Thus ended one hippie's excursion into free enterprise. His departure was unmourned, according to this *Tribune* editorial:

> Credit goes to the persons who showed enough interest to contact the police department about Redwood City's psychedelic newsboy.
>
> Protests came after the *Tribune* ran a story about an 18-year-old bearded youth peddling hippie-type newspapers at Broadway and El Camino Real.
>
> Many of the sales were made to students at Sequoia High School across the street. . . .
>
> The boy was told by police to fold up shop.
>
> We hope a way can be found to prevent a reappearance by this boy or some other hippie-type from making sales from our streets. The hippies we can do without.
>
> It's nice to know we have people who are willing to get involved by letting the police know that they frown upon activities such as were being conducted by the psychedelic newsboy.

Speaking Up for Freedom

The field of journalism is littered with the bones of people like Feyler—bums, visionaries, radicals, and conservatives alike—yet some of the most libertarian interpretations of the First Amendment have been made on behalf of unsavory journalists. The *Saturday Press* of Minneapolis, for example, was a scurrilous, anti-Semitic sheet that oozed vituperation. In 1927, after one of its several smears of city officials the Hennepin county attorney halted the paper's publication under what came to be known as the "Minnesota Gag Law." Many righteous individuals were relieved to hear the last of the paper, but Robert R. McCormick of the ultraconservative Chicago *Tribune* rose to its defense. Perceiving a threat to *all* newspapers, McCormick financed the *Saturday Press's* appeal to the United States Supreme Court—and the *Press* won. Speaking for the majority, Chief Justice Charles Evans Hughes found the Minnesota law unconstitutional, and in so doing held that the First Amendment protected newspapers from state, as well as federal, suppression.

Nine days after Feyler retired from the newspaper business, the Redwood City press council, which had been established five months earlier, met in monthly session. Its agenda called attention to the newsboy episode and asked if the *Tribune* had "engaged in a community-minded activity, or was the paper a party to suppression?"

The nine press council members assembled in the private dining room of a Redwood City restaurant that is a favorite of service clubs were an interesting cross section: a school custodian, a city councilwoman, a painter's union business representative, a high school newspaper editor, a trial lawyer, a housewife, a social science teacher, a J. C. Penney store manager, and a retired junior high math teacher. Also present were *Tribune* publisher Ray Spangler and editor Dave Schutz and the two university researchers, myself and William L. Rivers.

It was typical of the Redwood City council to approach the topic gingerly. One member wanted to know what was meant by "underground" newspapers. Greg Herman, the high school newspaper editor, provided an answer: A nonestablishment "free" press. Al Hinners, the custodian, thought the word might relate to "underworld," and then recalled the gangster days of Prohibition.

To myself and Dr. Rivers it seemed clear that the *Tribune*, the would-be vigilantes, and the police had erred. Couldn't the council see

William B. Blankenburg, a former newspaper reporter and editor, is Associate Professor of Journalism and Mass Communication at the University of Wisconsin. He served as secretary to the Bend and Redwood City press councils.

that? Mary Henderson, the city councilwoman and an ardent libertarian, had been rankled by the police action, but for a forthright
woman, she began rather tentatively: "I think there are several
questions involved here." Then, with calculated innocence, she asked:
"Who has the right to decide? What if the big San Francisco papers
decided that the *Tribune* is an underground paper and therefore should
be run off the street? In this case, should the *Tribune* have the right to
decide?"

The implication was clear. Byron Skinner, the Sequoia High
School teacher, said he was absolutely opposed to violations of press
freedom, adding that: "I definitely feel that these papers have some
value for the young people, and better than suppressing them we should
try to understand them."

"Now wait a minute," Hinners said. Although he had some
long-standing complaints about the *Tribune*, he began to defend the
newspaper. "There are certain requirements that you have to abide by
in order to publish a paper. That one [Feyler's] didn't go through the
proper channels in order to hit the streets."

Before the others could respond, *Tribune* publisher Ray Spangler
cut into the argument. Both he and editor Schutz were uncomfortable.
Spangler was a past president of Sigma Delta Chi, the national
professional journalistic society, and a former director of the Associated Press. Schutz had served on Sigma Delta Chi's Freedom of
Information Committee, and in 1967-68 he was president of the
Associated Press Managing Editors Association. Both were chagrined by
their newspaper's attitude toward Feyler. "The editorial takes an
indefensible position," Spangler said. "All I can say is that it happened.
The *Tribune* has no right to run anyone off the street."

He explained that the editorial had been written by a zealous
staffer and published while he and Schutz were attending a convention.
Although disavowing the editorial's position, Spangler took responsibility for it. "It's our baby," he said, "but it sure looks strange right
now." He did, however, defend the news story that prompted the
incident: "I think we ran it correctly."

A Jousting Match

Not long before, I had watched another press council take a
publisher to task. The newly formed press council of Bend, Oregon, was
testing its role as advisor to the *Bulletin*, which is owned and edited by

Robert W. Chandler. Mrs. Harriet Langmas, an attractive housewife in her mid-thirties, was about to challenge Chandler regarding his paper's slender coverage of the Bend Community Concerts Association. Mrs. Langmas is one of the city's leading piano teachers and an advocate of Community Concerts, which brings musical culture to the hinterlands. Bend is 160 miles from Portland and 128 from Eugene—distances that are magnified by the intervening Cascades. With its population of 13,200, its mountain backdrop, and its cool green parks along the banks of the lovely Deschutes River, Bend might well be most Americans' ideal small city. But because of its isolation and limited population, it is not a cultural center, and Mrs. Langmas felt that itinerant performers ought to be warmly welcomed and fully promoted in the 8500-circulation *Bulletin*.

She and other Community Concerts supporters were disappointed with the routine story on a membership drive published in the *Bulletin*. "I attended a meeting yesterday," Mrs. Langmas said, "and when I arrived everybody was saying, "Let's parboil Chandler. His Bend *Bulletin* is for the birds and there is no way we can ever build up the arts with the *Bulletin* as our only paper.""

"Start another one," Chandler suggested.

"I know," Mrs. Langmas laughed, "that's just what you'd tell them. But they were very concerned. They were upset because they were so eager to get the new people in town to join, and they couldn't get a story they had written into the paper."

Chandler said that the story did get into the paper, although as is the custom of the *Bulletin* and most other newspapers, the handout had been rewritten.

Mrs. Langmas also had an earlier bone to pick. "Last May, when Whittemore and Lowe were here, we were absolutely shocked by the turnout. Here was probably the foremost piano team in America and we got no story, no picture, and yet both of these things were supplied to the *Bulletin*. The picture was a glossy—a handout—and my big criticism is, why not put in a picture?" Chandler referred this time to statistics. Every day, he said, the *Bulletin* receives 70,000 words from United Press International, another 70,000 in handouts, and up to 25,000 in local copy—all of which has to be pared to fit a news hole of 40,000 words in a typical twelve-page issue.

"I'm still not sold," Mrs. Langmas said. "The same day that the concert publicity should have appeared there were stories on seven tornadoes and four convicted criminals, and lots of wirephotos."

At this point Chandler began deprecating the motives of Community Concerts, which he characterized as "another commercial branch of the Columbia Broadcasting System." (He was right about the profit motive but wrong about CBS; the parent of Community Concerts is Columbia Artists Management, no kin to the Columbia Broadcasting System.) Mrs. Langmas remained firm. "Did you know that we pay half as much for our concerts in Bend as anyone else because we're trying to stay alive and we'll probably have concerts for only one more year? In other words, the average star attraction, like the Lee Evans Jazz Trio, should be earning $1300. Just to keep the Bend Community Concerts Association alive they will appear for only $600. Did you know that?" Surprised by her own fervor, she laughed.

"No," Chandler said, "and I don't see that it makes a great deal of difference."

Mrs. Langmas took another tack. She charged the *Bulletin* with neglecting all the arts while devoting at least a page a day to sports when "not everyone is interested in sports." Chandler replied that other local artists and other specialized groups such as naturalists and rockhounds appeared to be satisfied with *their* coverage. Another press council member, Mrs. Ruth Burleigh, observed that her group, Arts Now, was not unhappy. Mike Hollern, the young business manager of Brooks-Scanlon Lumber Company, the town's largest employer, added that "the paper does a good job. This [the Community Concerts issue] may be an isolated instance where publicity is incomplete. But we had quite a successful music festival last summer." He noted that the *Bulletin*—with Brooks-Scanlon—had been a principle guarantor of a symphony concert.

"I may have to backtrack a bit," Mrs. Langmas conceded, but then she saw another route to coverage: reviews of performances. "When an artist performs here, I like to read what's thought about that person. How about the *Oregonian*? How do the Portland papers do their reviews? What motive—?"

"The reason we don't run reviews is that we don't have anyone we think is qualified to write them," Chandler said. "Our position has not changed in the years I've been here. We have roughly one full-time news person for every 1000 readers. The *Oregonian* has one for about every 2500, but they've got so many more people that they can find somebody who's knowledgeable on music, for example, and who'll meet their deadlines."

"Have you ever tried to find anyone like this?"

"Yes, we have. It's hard to find competent people who meet our basic copy standards, who will work on schedule, and who'll have the copy in by eight o'clock the next morning."

The moderator, Dr. Rivers, cited similar problems occurring in other small cities where a newspaper has good reporters but none who qualifies as a critic. Another member, Liz Holbrook, wondered if the *Bulletin* might not skip the reviewing task and simply do a personality feature on the visiting performer. Turning to Mrs. Langmas, she said, "Maybe your organization isn't establishing rapport with the newspaper. Perhaps if you invited one of the staff to attend, he might become interested."

"We do send the newspaper complimentary tickets every time," Mrs. Langmas said, "but no one on the staff has joined the Association."

Chandler laughed. "Why buy the cow when the milk is free?"

"Well, right," Mrs. Langmas said, "We'd love to have you come for nothing, just come."

"But nobody wants to come," Chandler said, "that's the point. Even with free tickets nobody comes."

Mrs. Langmas circled back to the subject of pictures. If the reporters don't want to come to a concert, and if the photographer doesn't work at night, then why not use a good glossy photo provided by the Community Concerts Association? Chandler said that the *Bulletin*, which had converted to the offset printing process a year earlier, was finicky about picture quality, and that extreme care in lighting and darkroom techniques was required. "We often get arty shots from organizations like Community Concerts, and these are contrasty and just don't reproduce well."

Press council member Gordon Robberson saw a solution: "Bob, why don't you set up standards for publicity pictures? When people ask you for photographic coverage and you don't have a photographer available, simply hand them a sheet that specifies your photographic standards."

Chandler didn't think this would work. "We'll take a look at anybody's picture," he said, "but the standards are too hard to define."

Sensing that the topic had been exhausted, Dr. Rivers suggested that the council turn to other issues. The discussion of publicity, he said, may have caused Chandler to become sensitive to feelings of which he had not been aware. But Dr. Rivers added, "We don't direct him; we make suggestions and get answers from him. And I hope that some of you are more sensitive to his kinds of problems, too." This was one of several occasional reminders to the councils of the ground rule that they had no power to force change on the newspaper.

The publisher, of course, was *free from* having to accept criticisms or suggestions, yet *free to* decide what was valuable and what was dross. Chandler never did improve his opinion of Community Concerts, nor did he begin to send his photographers out at night or write reviews of artistic performances. However, Mrs. Langmas was ecstatic to find a later concert mentioned on page one, and Chandler did reconsider the comments on photographic standards: a few weeks later he produced a memorandum for publicity chairmen. This did not mean that the *Bulletin* would accept all pictures that met the criteria; instead, the written specifications stemmed the flow of fuzzy pictures and made clear to publicists the quality of pictures that *might* be accepted.

The Councils Discover Complexities

The eighteen members of the Redwood City and Bend press councils cared a great deal about overcoming their understandable ignorance of the journalistic process. "Who puts the headlines on stories?" "How many reporters do you have?" "Who covers Prineville?" "How much does a syndicated feature cost?" "What is your policy on juvenile names?"

Their inquisitiveness was demonstrated as the Bend council reconnoitered a seemingly simple question: In a story of an auto accident, does the phrase "while trying to turn" imply recklessness? Early on a wet October morning in Bend, a sailor on leave missed a corner near his home and crashed into a house. No one was injured. The *Bulletin* carried a picture of the damage and a brief story that opened with a humorous reference to the home-owner's consternation upon finding an automobile on his porch. The sailor's parents were highly distressed and went to editor Chandler, who told the council of their complaint. The parents felt the *Bulletin* had implied reckless speeding by saying the boy was "trying to turn" instead of simply "turning" a corner. The parents wanted Chandler to print a correction they had composed which applauded the young sailor for serving his country.

As was typical in the small city of Bend, most of the council members knew of the family and were familiar with the accident site.

Yet they still had many questions. Where does the *Bulletin* get its facts in a case like this? From the police blotter, Chandler said. Are the police usually accurate? Yes, in his experience. Was the boy actually turning or did he run straight off the road? Were there any witnesses? Who was the investigating officer? Was he new to the force? Did the *Bulletin* run a later story on the boy? What is the *Bulletin's* policy on retractions? Do people really notice such attributions as "according to police" or do they blame the newspaper? Is the lead of the story good, or is it too flippant? Would the lead be appropriate if there had been injuries? Did anyone outside of the family complain? Did the blotter say anything about wet streets? Eventually the council agreed that the phrase was dubious, and expressed mixed emotions about feature leads on accident stories.

In both Redwood City and Bend, the publishers were surprised and somewhat disappointed with the councils' extensive information-seeking. They had expected reactions, not questions. Obviously some of the queries were a means of postponing judgment; a member who did not care to take a position could defer his opinion by posing a question. But most of the questions were sincere and pertinent. The members were quicker to recognize the information gap than the publishers. Charged with evaluating responsible performance in a newspaper, the members wished to be responsible themselves by not finding fault without facts or making recommendations without reasons.

As the councils grew more knowledgeable about journalistic techniques, their quest for information diminished—but never ceased entirely. No sooner had the members acquired an inkling of why a newspaper won't accept color slides than they were faced with the complexities of territorial rights to syndicated features. The effect was sobering, like laboring up a hill only to find another summit ahead. Here were eighteen intelligent, concerned citizens who valued journalism highly, and who came to realize they knew very little about its inner workings. They discovered that practical reasons could excuse many shortcomings and foil most desirable changes. Economic and technical impediments were mutually frustrating to the members and the publishers.

It seemed surprising that the technology of journalism should intrude so often in what were supposed to be ethical deliberations. After all, the ground rules of journalism might well be summed up in three words—accuracy, adequacy, and fairness—and the Canons of Journalism, promulgated by the American Society of Newspaper Editors, are only sixteen paragraphs long. But almost all ethical considerations in journalism, of course, are entangled in technical and economic problems. Then too, the journalistic ground rules, while simple, are not simple to apply. Is a newspaper more adequate if its coverage is "deep"? What, then, does depth mean for objectivity? And for breadth? What must be skimped to save space? The dilemmas were numerous, and the West Coast councils became wary of facile solutions. They developed a judicial stance, hesitating to prosecute or exhort.

Judges, Not Prosecutors

It is conceivable that a press council might style itself as an agitator, provocateur, evangelist, or crusader. We asked the council members if they would like to form investigative subcommittees. Some interest was shown, but the members preferred to have the issues raised by the publisher, the moderator, or by a complaining reader. The Redwood City council was asked if it might crusade for freedom of information under California's Brown Act, an open-meeting law. Would the council be interested in seeking writs of mandamus or injunction against secretive public officials? Byron Skinner, the Redwood City teacher, thought that litigation might be appropriate activity for a national but not a local press council. "Wouldn't we be casting ourselves in the role of busybody?" Tim Kelly, the Redwood City painters' union representative, argued that a council *might* attempt to pry open meetings, but only after urging the newspaper to take the lead. The council consensus seemed best expressed by William Keogh. As a trial lawyer, he was no stranger to adversary proceedings, but he saw a more detached role for community press councils:

> I hesitate to think that a press council would ever do more than what this body does. My own view is that any time it went beyond its functions as a deliberative, thoughtful, advisory body, a council would ultimately destroy itself. As I see it, a council is to give a newspaper careful viewpoints worked out in a reasonable, congenial atmosphere. The council's relationship to a newspaper is as counselor, understander, listener, sounding board, and

critic. As I see this body, its charm and its use is that all of us people of different backgrounds get together to answer questions about what a newspaper should do. To selectively take up the cudgels for this or that cause would weaken our effectiveness. Our judicial cap, so to speak, would have been taken off.

As amateur judges working with the inchoate common law of journalism, the press council members were cautious as they faced the task of rendering some fairly sophisticated decisions. The Bend council tackled the problem of rebuttals to letters from readers. On many newspapers, the editor will often use his letters as a springboard to a free-swinging editorial. Many editors append biting notes to readers' letters. This was the case in Bend until 1953 when Chandler acquired the *Bulletin* and immediately began a policy of not refuting letters unless they contained an important factual error. His decision was not easy. Argumentative by nature, Chandler enjoys rough-and-tumble debate. But he also knows the value of letters and the sensitivity of a rural audience. By his accounting, he has broken his rule only four times in his fifteen years with the *Bulletin*. One breach occurred during the press council experience, much to the concern of his council.

A Bend teacher, Ken Cooper, wrote the *Bulletin* to complain that Chandler, in his role as a member of the Oregon Board of Education, advocated less academic freedom for high school teachers than for college teachers. Chandler refuted the charge in an editorial.

The council worried not so much over the merits of the argument as about the effects of Chandler's response on Bend citizens who might refrain from writing out of fear of counterattack. As Gordon Robberson put it, "In almost any community with a good newspaper and an intelligent publisher like Bob, there is a certain amount of restraint by the public in its expression, its action, because of the editor. I think that some of us will not say what we truly and deeply feel—that we will not write a letter to the editor—because of a concern of being 'taken on' by the editor. The man, by the very nature of his job, wields a tremendous power."

Robberson was accurate about fear of the publisher. At 46, Chandler still possessed the physique of a football lineman. In his office hangs a symbolic mace, gift of a friend. He chews tobacco, swallows the juice, and mows his hair with an electric razor (a friend observed that he'd bite it off if he could only reach it). People in Bend typically say that other people in Bend are afraid of Chandler.

Even though the editors of many papers comment on letters, the council felt the practice inappropriate in Bend. After Robberson's remarks, member Robert Foley, a circuit court judge, recalled, "Maybe the people here learned over the years that it doesn't pay to write letters. The editor before Mr. Chandler was Robert W. Soyer, and if letters didn't agree with him, he took you on right then and there. Anyone who had sense didn't write to the editor at all. Even now the people are very concerned; they feel like they are taking on Goliath. The newspaper is a powerful instrumentality."

Returning to the issue of the Cooper letter, Robberson remarked, "It seems we feel that Chandler more or less chastises this man [Cooper] for writing the letter. It seems personal. In a sense he's told this man he's wrong, that he's ignorant."

"But didn't it start out as a personal conflict between the two men?" Mrs. Langmas asked. "Cooper happens to be president of the state teachers' organization." Her point was that *two* Goliaths were involved—Chandler as a member of the Board of Education and Cooper as a teachers' official. She wondered if this might not justify a departure from the *Bulletin's* rule.

"Well," Robberson said, "based on that, maybe Chandler should have answered the letter."

"They were both writing as representatives of organizations," Dr. William Guyer agreed.

Raymond Hickman, a truck driver, framed the council's decision: "I can't see that he was out of line in answering this particular letter. But I'd sure hate to see him start a policy of answering all letters."

Free to Disagree

Just before the first working meeting of the Redwood City press council, *Tribune* publisher Ray Spangler took me aside. "Where did you get all those union people?" he asked. He was referring to members Tim Kelly, business representative for the Brotherhood of Painters and Decorators, and Al Hinners, Sequoia High School head custodian and president of Local 57 of the American Federation of State, County, City, and Municipal Employees. Spangler's concern was not unusual for a publisher. After twenty-two years of dealing with labor as a boss and adversary, he was unaccustomed to receiving editorial advice from union men.

I told Spangler we had recruited the members with a cross section in mind—or as close to one as possible with only nine people. Because San Mateo County, of which Redwood City is the seat, is heavily unionized, we applied to the Central Labor Council for names of interested working people. Other members were also recruited from organizations such as the county bar association and the school system, or reached through personal acquaintances in Redwood City.

Spangler and editor Schutz had recently suffered from labor strife. Union relations had been amicable enough within the plant (Peninsula papers are rarely struck; San Francisco newspaper settlements often set the pattern for the suburbs). But in October 1967 the Teamsters picketed the *Tribune* plant in an apparent effort to organize *Tribune* circulation drivers. The newspaper immediately petitioned the National Labor Relations Board for an election, but the Teamsters said they weren't really interested in organization. The *Tribune* then gained a temporary injunction prohibiting the Teamsters from having more than five pickets on hand. The infighting continued by means of pamphlets from both sides, but it was a mystifying episode, since the Teamsters never made it clear what they were actually seeking. (Spangler guessed that what they really wanted was to organize the *Tribune's* larger sister paper, the Palo Alto *Times*.)

In this context, Spangler was understandably sensitive to union members on the press council, and that night's agenda asked for an evaluation of the *Tribune's* coverage of its labor problems. This provided for a clear test of labor solidarity on the council. Both Kelly and Hinners were old enough to remember hard times for labor in San Mateo County, and Hinners in particular had a tendency to shoot from the hip on labor matters. (To him, Ronald Reagan was unfit to be governor because Reagan, who had once been the liberal president of the Screen Actors Guild, had become conservative and "turned against his own union.") Yet Hinners' reaction to the agenda item was surprising: "Could I say something on this? The Teamsters were out of order in picketing the *Tribune*. In San Mateo County, every plan to picket should come before the Central Labor Council, and the Teamsters' didn't."

Somewhat taken aback, Dr. Rivers asked if the Central Labor

Council would go so far as to help the *Tribune* management prevent such picketing. "We did notify the Teamsters about this through the labor council," Hinners replied, "but we can't step in on Spangler's behalf unless he requests it." And if Spangler did make such a request? "Then the Council would issue publicity against the Teamster picketing. We would inform the locals that the picketing was not sanctioned. I would suggest that Mr. Spangler get in touch with the president of the Central Labor Council—a phone call would do it—and he'd have action next Monday night."

Hinners' promise of Labor Council assistance against the Teamsters, who did not belong to the Council (Kelly commented wryly that Teamsters tend to go their own way), was no assurance that picketing would end—but it seemed a far cry from a labor gang-up on the *Tribune* via the press council.

Even as Spangler discovered something about the myth of labor solidarity in a press council meeting, so did the union men learn something about intransigence in the press. Just before another meeting, Tim Kelly diffidently approached me with a *Tribune* story he wanted to have discussed "if there is time." I assured him that time would be taken; members' topics had the highest priority. The story which was published in the news columns was headlined *How to Keep Unions Away from the Door,* with no attribution and no quotation marks, just as though the paper were issuing instructions. It was a report of an anti-union speech made to the Western Electronics Manufacturers' Association by a Palo Alto attorney who urged, among other things, that managers "carefully screen job applicants for troublemakers. Check with their former employers. During their probationary period check their attitudes. If one is incompetent, fire him."

The fifteen-inch story was little more than a polemic topped by an unattributed, one-sided quote, but Kelly was not greatly exercised. "The man has a perfect right to his anti-union views," he said —then adding with a smile, "The story contained some useful information for labor, too." As Kelly spoke, Spangler reread the story with a deepening frown. "I'm inclined to agree that there's a flaw in the headline. It implies that the *Tribune* is offering a primer to management on how to combat union organization. Qualification was needed. In fact, I don't know why the hell we devoted so much space to the story."

Other divergent attitudes were apparent. Two politically conservative* members divided sharply in their views of the *Tribune's* relationship with the mercantile establishment. One privately assured me that the *Tribune* had succumbed to "downtown influences." The next day, and quite independently, the other conservative confided that the *Tribune* was badly biased *against* downtown merchants because the paper had failed to "accentuate the positive qualities of the business district."

Nor did husband and wife necessarily agree during a press council meeting, as demonstrated at a final Redwood City session to which spouses had been invited. The topic of racial identification arose, and Byron Skinner, the only black member, said he had mixed emotions but generally went along with the customary newspaper practice of identifying race only when pertinent to the story. "I disagree!" Mrs. Skinner broke in. "I think black people need to be identifiable by other black persons in *all* things. I know I would like to be identified in the paper as a black person in a story of crime or anything else." The council was fascinated, and Dr. Rivers asked, "Well, what *is* the feeling in the black community?" Skinner smiled at his wife. "Every community has several voices," he said.

The disagreement heard throughout was recognized as valuable by publisher Spangler and inherently less dangerous than his previous panel of merchant-advisors, which he termed "a power-structure press council." He added, "nothing came of it because we weren't really talking to our readers. But this present type of press council has great possibilities, and has been a great benefit to the *Tribune*. It gives the newspaper a sense of direct accountability and responsibility."

The Publishers Didn't Play Dead

But a bit of well-placed bellicosity went a long way with the press councils, and Chandler knew when to fire a salvo. Mrs. Langmas once zeroed in on Chandler's policy against night photography. Why couldn't he at least send out his fine young photographer to snap visiting

---

*In the first thirty minutes of the first Redwood City meeting, every member had volunteered his political affiliation. A discussion of Shirley Temple Black's political aptitude—she was then running for Congress—was a strong stimulant. The results: four Republicans, three Democrats, and two independents. San Mateo County had registration percentages of 54 Democratic, 42 Republican, and 4 independent.

performers? "Who determines that policy? I've heard lots of criticism of it," she asked.

"I determine that, completely and absolutely," Chandler said, glowering. "We do send reporters to night meetings, maybe fifteen or twenty meetings a week, and they get an afternoon off if they have to go out at night. We do report meetings if public money is being spent or the community is somehow affected." Warming up, he continued: "But the only guy we've got who can take a decent picture is Dave Swan, and he gets to work at seven o'clock in the morning. I'll be a son of a bitch if I'll send him out at night to take pictures of the Daughters of I-Will-Arise—or Community Concerts, for that matter." The council moved to other matters.

Later Mrs. Langmas criticized Chandler's policy of not printing "thank you" letters. A large group of adults had volunteered to teach young people how to water-ski. "Here were all these adults, and all these kids," Mrs. Langmas complained, "and one young man stayed up all night writing a letter of gratitude to publish in the *Bulletin* and—"

"And he'll never get it in the paper, either. We never run thank-you letters."

"I know, but—"

"*And we ain't going to!*"

"Bob, aren't you ever shocked by *anything*?" Mrs. Langmas protested, feeling considerable shock herself.

Chandler laughed. "The real reason behind the policy, of course, is that someone always has a Sunday school picnic and writes a long letter to the editor thanking the Pepsi-Cola Company for seven cans of pop."

"But this wasn't commercialism."

"In my opinion it would be a hell of a lot better manners on the kids' part to write a letter to the people who took them to the reservoir. We're not going to aid their laziness by printing their letters."

The publishers could often turn back criticism by requesting particulars. When a Redwood City member off-handedly suggested the *Tribune* was not giving as much attention to leftist opinions as to conservative views, Spangler said, "You'll have to give us an example of that." Having no example at hand, the member did not pursue the question.

All this is not to suggest the publishers consistently responded with bared fangs. More often, they disarmed their councils with wit. At an early meeting, Spangler deftly deflated his council by reciting a pointed couplet:

> In all our towns and all our cities,
> There are no statues to committees.

The publishers were not averse to telling anecdotes reflecting on themselves. Spangler recalled a train-car accident story that was so garbled the engineer was reported driving the car. Chandler confessed that this classified ad once slipped into the *Bulletin*: "Frank, come back. Bring two rings, teething and wedding." Such anecdotes reminded the councils that they were examining the work of a fallible human institution. As Spangler remarked at his first meeting, "The *Tribune* should be thought of as people. We have 153 employees, and we're bound to make mistakes."

If a publisher is sensitive to outside intrusions—and most publishers are very sensitive indeed—he may set additional ground rules for his council. At first Chandler wanted nothing said about his editorial page because he regarded it as the editor's preserve. Later, as he grew more familiar with his council and realized his strengths, he brought up several editorial-page topics, including the difficulty of making choices between syndicated columnists and establishing a policy on letters to the editor. Spangler wished to avoid even the appearance of outside control by the council. Hardly anyone in the general public or on the *Tribune* staff knew of its existence. In Bend, however, occasional news stories covered the council and invited public inquiries.

On one occasion in Bend, a news story involved the *Bulletin* itself. This occurred when a reporter who was leaving the paper, a California girl who had just finished eighteen months as an intern, was packing to return home when Bend police arrested her for possession of marijuana.

Chandler faced a peculiar problem. Certainly the arrest should be reported (along with two others made the same day). But what emphasis should be given to the girl's connection with the *Bulletin*? He drew an analogy from a personal policy: if any member of the Chandler family (he has six lively children) should be arrested for anything, the story would go on page one. Thus, the three arrests were reported at the top of the front page under the headline *Bend Drug Arrests Made as More Are Expected.* The story began: "Seven months of undercover investigation resulted in arrests for three Bend residents, including a former Bulletin reporter, on narcotics charges late Friday." The name of the former reporter and her dates of service with the *Bulletin* were given.

Chandler asked the Bend council for an evaluation of the story. The members agreed that the case was properly handled, but one warned, "If the story had been buried on page five, then we'd *really* have something to argue about." Chandler raised another question. Just before the arrest he had written several letters of recommendation for the girl to other publishers. What now is his responsibility to those newspapers? Should he write again, mentioning the arrest? The council felt that Chandler's responsibility to the journalistic profession required him to write a second letter. "Thanks," he said. "I did."

A strength of the publishers was their authority as journalistic experts. Both had long experience as working newsmen as well as executives. Chandler had been a journalist in Denver and Los Angeles (he is not related to the Chandler publishing family of the Los Angeles *Times*) before acquiring the *Bulletin* in 1953. Spangler joined the *Tribune* in 1937 as a reporter, becoming editor and publisher in 1945; four years later he turned the editorship over to David Schutz.

Nor were the publishers deficient in general knowledge. Spangler is well known for his fund of Redwood City history and for his investigations of shady business practices (he has written several illuminating columns as the "lucky winner" of a sewing machine). Chandler is a keen student of law, and recently wrote an article on the Oregon Judicial Council for the *Oregon Law Review*. Like all good journalists, the two executives had experiences and information that ranged far beyond the confines of their profession. When a Redwood City council member asked if the *Tribune* might not start a campaign to preserve a cluster of old tannery buildings, Spangler outlined the historic and financial value of the site, then added, without much nostalgia, what it was like to work with hides, as he had in his youth. He concluded, dryly, that "it's not much to get romantic about." In Bend, during a discussion of coverage of civil proceedings, Chandler reported matter-of-factly that there had been no prosecutions for adultery in Oregon for fifteen years.

Occasionally the members found themselves inundated by data. Responding to a criticism that the *Bulletin* left ink smudges on the hands of its readers, Chandler commented on the nature of the offset printing process, the cost ratio between letterpress and offset ink, the composition of ink and its rate of absorption, the relative inkiness of pictures over type, and the proportionate cost of ink to newsprint. He added that the *Bulletin* was nearly banned from a local hospital because of excessive ink shortly after its conversion to offset.

Usually such details arose from a pertinent context, and the members were often fascinated. They agreed that in accident stories a newspaper should avoid imputations of guilt simply by saying the cars collided instead of reporting that one car struck another. They did not know, until the publisher told them, that the first-mentioned driver might assume *he* is being blamed—and there is no way in a narrative to present the names simultaneously.

Because the two West Coast publishers possessed generous stores of knowledge, particularly on journalistic matters, and because of their willingness to share it, they were accorded their strongest defense against usurpation of their freedom: respect.

Was Freedom Abridged?

When the Bend and Redwood City councils reached the end of their prescribed terms, the publishers were interviewed separately. The discussions covered the range of council affairs—from recruitment of members to newspaper policy decisions. Because of the sensitivity of the press, I deemed one question crucial: "Do you feel that your freedom was in any way abridged by your press council?"

The answer from both men was the same: a warm chuckle. They did not relinquish their freedom, nor had their councils tried to take it.

CHAPTER THREE

Press Councils
and Press Responsibility

by WILLIAM B. BLANKENBURG

> Liberty means responsibility. That is why
> most men dread it.
> —George Bernard Shaw

Perhaps for the first time in their lives, the council members in Bend and Redwood City encountered such petty but potent stumbling blocks as headline counting and copyfitting, two basic routines of the journalist. Member Al Hinners came to a Redwood City council meeting with this *Tribune* headline: *For New Sequoia School: Wall to Wall Carpets?* The headline appeared on the eve of a school-bond election, and in Hinners' opinion it suggested fiscal irresponsibility. The bond issue had failed; Hinners blamed the headline. In the leisure of hindsight, his fellow members tinkered with improvements. "What about *Economy Move in School Construction*?" Byron Skinner suggested after hearing Hinners assert that carpeting is cheaper in the long run than linoleum. Mary Henderson had another idea: "*Board of Education Aims Toward Improved School Facilities.*"

Spangler laughed sympathetically. He had wrestled with tight headline space throughout his professional life; moreover, he knew the coercive power of journalistic standards. Even though the *Tribune* editorially favored the bond issue, it could not suppress the fact that the school's trustees had spent the bulk of their preelection meeting arguing the merits of wall-to-wall carpets. Mrs. Henderson got the point. She recalled yet another election eve when the district's teachers confronted the trustees with demands for higher wages. Again the *Tribune* was constrained to report the event, and again the voters rebelled against new bonds.

Why Can't You Do More?

Operating under a news ethic, with a rule that says "If it happens, we'll print it," newspapermen typically reject the idea that they should suppress news "for the good of the public." They feel the public is better off with information than without it. But they are trapped between their standards and their limitations—between the rule of disclosure and their physical and financial inability to cover everything in sight—and the diametric pressures can be great, as the two councils soon learned. Generally the councils did not wish to remove anything from the newspapers, but to add, and they came to share some of the publishers' distresses.

When the *Tribune* was criticized for favoring sports events over other school activities, editor Schutz replied, "We agree with you that some of these classroom activities, whether geography, science, math, or whatever, are extremely interesting. But obviously no newspaper can staff every classroom. We *can* staff football games and school board meetings, and we do." A bit later Spangler commiserated with Mrs. Henderson when she observed, "A partial stock-market list isn't very satisfactory. I'm happy that the *Tribune* carries some stocks, but I wish that it could carry the full report."

"This material has to come by Data-Speed," Spangler said, "and that's $200 a week. Then to set the full list, we would need two more linotype tape machines. If we could afford it, we'd do it. We'd *like* to do it, but we're not quite there yet. We also have a production jam and barely manage to get out the present list on two machines. The stocks are the last thing to go into the paper. We have to hold the press until 2:15 P.M. to get them in, and we need to get our paper out early."

"Why do you have to deliver so early?" Mrs. Henderson asked, intimating that a full stock list might be published if the deadline was later.

"Our last delivery is supposed to be no later than 5:30. We think the paper is dead by dinner time, particularly with the women readers. Television begins to take over then, and in suburbia we have many evening meetings and other events. We want to get into the homes early enough so that the housewife can read the paper before she cooks dinner."

As for the necessary capital, Spangler sketched a gloomy picture. He observed that a recent San Francisco newspaper strike settlement "was a pretty tough financial package that resulted immediately in raised advertising rates in San Francisco. This put a squeeze on some big advertisers, and there may be less money left over for suburban papers. We expect a pretty tight economic squeeze on the industry. Some of the advertisers are beginning to think of alternatives to newspapers. We're caught. It's hard to improve the product right now in terms of additional news space and personnel."

To some members, the obstacles to change seemed endless, and a Bend participant eventually unburdened himself: "Here are my frustrations in a nutshell. We can't discuss the front page because it is a package from UPI. We can't discuss the editorial page because it is the personal baby of the editor. The local news can't be covered in more depth because there are only so many reporters and photographers."

Actually, he and his fellow members had talked about all these things and more. What they often found, and what was at the base of his complaint, was an apparently unchippable crust of encumbrances.

The *Bulletin's* editorial page was clearly acknowledged as Chandler's preserve, but the council trod there to condemn rebuttals to readers' letters and to evaluate the substitution of columnist Arthur Hoppe for Barry Goldwater. Here, too, certain realities intruded. Chandler would like to publish Russell Baker's column, but he could not afford to buy the full New York *Times* wire service to get Baker. Art Buchwald was another possibility, but he appeared in the Portland *Oregonian.*

As for the UPI "package," the *Bulletin* was generous with its space by most standards, averaging 60 percent news or features to 40 percent advertising (most dailies, including the *Tribune*, reverse the percentages). Still there is a limit on the amount of news space that can be supported economically, and usually less than a third of the UPI's daily transmission to Bend found room in the *Bulletin* (the council had ample opportunity to argue about *which* third ought to be published).

As the council discovered, the out-of-town report could have been expanded, but only with some reduction in local coverage. And local coverage could have been deepened—as the *Bulletin* demonstrated with a cogent series on Bend's five black residents—at the expense of breadth. The members grappled reluctantly with the question of which local reports, such as routine accident stories, might be condensed to make room. But they began to wonder, as James Thurber once did, "Which is trivial, the diamond or the elephant?" Is the community better served by extensive coverage of most events or by fewer and longer stories on trends and problems? What is the recipe for an appropriate mix?

Out of such conundrums grew press council headaches—and a measure of sympathy for the newspapers. Byron Skinner, often skeptical of *Tribune* performance, commented, "Criticizing is easy, but reporting is a good deal harder than I thought."

Then too, the members were faced with publishers who often seemed to have tried everything and to know everything. Particularly in a small city where the publisher takes an active part in the news process, as Chandler did, does his knowledgeability become a challenge to the council.

For example, at its April meeting the Bend council wondered whether pretrial publicity was a threat to due process in local courts. In the pretrial hearing of a manslaughter case, the defendant had cited a *Bulletin* editorial as prejudicial to his defense. Chandler argued to his council that no real problem existed because change of venue was usually granted in Deschutes County whenever a defendant requested it. Several members appeared skeptical, but member Robert Foley, the judge, remarked, "As a matter of fact, I have just granted a change in this case." Chandler laughed. "I knew you would. I did some checking and found that you've never failed to grant a venue petition in the last five years." "Is that right?" Foley exclaimed.

Next to publishing, Chandler's favorite study is jurisprudence. "Are juvenile offenders being sufficiently punished?" Dr. Bill Guyer asked at one meeting. The council was greatly concerned about Bend youth, and Guyer's family had just suffered its fifth bicycle theft. Guyer had been appalled when one of his children made the precocious remark, "Why not steal bikes? If you're caught you only get probation." He asked Chandler, "Is the juvenile judge too soft, and, if so, has the newspaper explored the subject?"

"Under state law, we're unable to find out the sentences in any juvenile case," Chandler said.

"Couldn't you at least report, for example, that there were ten juvenile cases last week, of which nine were given probation and the tenth—"

"No dispositions and no records available."

"Isn't there any way you can investigate this?"

"No. As a practical matter we can't, once it gets into the juvenile court."

"Can a grand jury get at those records?"

"No, they are sealed within the juvenile court."

About the only way a newspaper can help get rid of a "soft" juvenile judge—and "softness" is a matter of opinion, Chandler observed—is to oppose him for reelection at the end of his six-year term. But he added, "No lawyer in his right mind will run against a sitting judge who is *compos mentis*." The reason for so many probationary sentences, Chandler explained, was that central Oregon's reformatory, which he had visited, wasn't geared to rehabilitation. Another factor in sentencing, he said, is that "the juvenile judge is tremendously dependent upon staff work, unlike the circuit court judge who has the benefit of an adversary proceeding. The juvenile judge operates in a shadow area. The head of the juvenile department, a counselor, makes the basic recommendation for sentencing and I'd guess that ninety-nine times out of a hundred the judge goes along with it." He went on to compare Oregon's juvenile procedure with Montana's, which is more punitive. He concluded with an analysis of the recent effects of the U.S. Supreme Court decisions affecting the rights of juveniles.

He also had information on an enormous range of other topics, including film-making in Oregon. (He had driven a six-horse team and covered wagon across a river in the movie *How the West Was Won* while dressed as a frontier housewife.) He had a sharp interest in weather forecasting, and when Mrs. Harriet Langmas asked if the *Bulletin* couldn't print more complete weather reports, Chandler was full of the subject. "The trouble is—besides the fact that our weather changes every five minutes—is that forecasts are made up by the weather bureau in Portland between 9 P.M. and midnight, and we don't publish until four o'clock the next afternoon. Poor Phil Brogan, our former reporter, sat there for forty-three years trying to make the Portland forecasts look right, and it bothered him all forty-three years because it came out wrong more often than right." If that was the case, Mrs. Langmas asked, why couldn't an old-timer like Brogan simply look out the window and make his own forecasts? "We tried that for a while," Chandler recalled, "but he was farther off than the Portland bureau."

Another request was for a regular series of shopping tips for Bend's housewives. "We've tried this," Chandler said, "but there's only one source of fresh produce for Bend, except for Safeway, which has its own system, and that's Pacific Fruit and Produce. All of our grocers' variation in prices is usually limited to a cent a pound except for a few loss-leaders, or unless they bought badly last week and have a case of oranges left over. Besides, price isn't everything. An old hen at 26 cents a pound isn't as good a buy as a younger one with more usable meat at 28 cents a pound. Even if we knew that fresh produce such as strawberries had arrived at the Portland market, we still wouldn't know if the same produce will come to Bend."

In a similar vein, another member wondered if the *Bulletin* could do more in the area of consumer protection. "Once one of my younger reporters wanted to do a feature on the old controversy over price differences between generic and proprietary drugs. We drew up a list of local sources to interview, and it consisted of a couple of druggists and a few doctors who weren't really experts on the matter. Besides, they were not disinterested, and therefore were not good sources. We ran into another problem on available sources recently when we asked a local banker for the effect of gold outflow on interest rates. Unfortunately, our bankers are operating managers and not international monetary experts."

Attempting to find something new to tell Chandler about journalism was like shopping for a rich uncle's birthday present. What can a council do for a publisher who seems to have tried everything at least twice? For one thing, it can occasionally correct him, since not even publishers are infallible. For example, council member Ray Hickman, one-time fireman and later truck driver, corrected and amplified Chandler's information on the extent of union apprenticeship programs in Bend, and other members would also sometimes snatch a bent fact from the conversation and straighten it. On the whole, however, neither Chandler nor Spangler were faulty with facts. What was of more concern to the councils was whether their perceptions were clear and judgment wise. Here is where a community council's strength becomes apparent. Enlightened as a publisher may be, he is not likely to possess the experience and knowledge of all his counselors combined.

Middle-Class Myopia

Whether a member realized it or not, he came to the council as a representative of a constituency within the community, and some of the constituencies were not usually within the publisher's orbit. Newspaper executives are often accused of viewing the world from the nineteenth hole of their country club. One professor, Lewis Donohew of the University of Kentucky, once asked publishers of three Midwestern states to list their most respected acquaintances. Most frequently mentioned were merchants, lawyers, public officials, bankers, and generally persons who shared the publisher's political affiliation.[1] Thus, a cross-sectional council, as in Redwood City, breaks into that circle—and a more homogeneous council like Bend's is capable of wrenching itself free from middle-class myopia long enough to face social problems.

At a meeting attended by members' husbands and wives, the Bend council evaluated a two-part *Bulletin* story on the town's only black family (the father of which operated the city dump) and the three black students at a nearby community college. The purpose of the story, according to *Bulletin* managing editor Bill Yates, was to tell local readers what it was like to be black in Bend.

Member Hickman said he had talked to some laboring men who felt the paper was "stirring things up" by printing the series. The first thing they wanted to know, Hickman said, was, "What's Chandler trying to do now? Here these colored folks are living peacefully and no one's bothering them, and they are not bothering anyone, and now he's stirring up trouble."

"We thought there might be people who wouldn't like the story," Yates replied, "but that was not a consideration as far as running it or not. We were if anything looking ahead to the day when Bend will have more Negroes, and the community ought to be prepared for this."

Mrs. Langmas remarked that some of her friends said the most striking thing about the story was the black father's views on the way the community's attitude toward him had changed since the death of Dr. Martin Luther King.

Mrs. Hickman found the story enlightening. "I think articles like these are good," she said. "Several of the secretaries at the high school were born and raised right here in central Oregon—one girl says she has never been out of the state. She doesn't know how the other half lives. They had a long discussion on this article the other day. Many of them feel terribly innocent. They are kind of isolated here, and need to know more. When they watch the rioting on TV, to them it's like looking at a movie."

The moderator asked if the council would like to see more local stories on social problems. What about religious division in the community, for example?

Mrs. Langmas laughed. "Bend is the only place in the country where the Knights of Columbus and the Masons have joint parties. Actually, Oregon has lower church membership than any state in the union, and Bend has the lowest church membership of any city in the state."

The council explored other areas. Does the idyllic and prosperous community of Bend have minority or poverty problems of any scope? What about the Indians who live sixty miles north on the Warm Springs reservation?

Mrs. Langmas reported she had talked with a white official who had said, "Every morning I'm afraid the bubble will burst and I will find that things aren't as good as they seem to be on the reservation. Our Indians seem to be doing very well."

Dr. Guyer snorted. "You just talk to some of the *Indians* up there—some of the folks who don't have electricity, who were promised it years ago when the dam was built, and who are living in poverty."

"I never fail to take a side-trip through the reservation when we go to Portland," Mrs. Langmas said. "It's a good thing for us to do; it brings reality pretty close. But it *does* seem that some progress is being made."

"Here is where the *Bulletin* has some responsibility," Dr. Guyer said. "The poverty problem is nationwide and timely, and Bend does have prominent people who don't realize we have poverty here. A while back I got into a big argument with a couple of my buddies when I said there was poverty in Bend. Right away they wanted to bet me, and I took quite a browbeating. So I went to a Catholic priest, two Protestant ministers, and several other people around town. I asked, 'Where is the poverty in Bend? I want to take some rascals on a ride and show them.' We proved that there *is* poverty in Bend."

Liz Holbrook, the young executive secretary of the local Red Cross chapter, agreed: "Our community should know this. Before I came here, all I ever heard was what a lovely town this was, with such pretty parks, and its summer opera. But we have nothing to offer the poor people of this area if their houses burn down. We just don't have any money for them. There are definitely pockets of poverty here, and some real resentment over all the talk about how marvelously neat the community is, and the parks we're fixing up, when we cannot help people with some of their basic problems."

"This Is a Revelation"

Not all of the constituency contributions were so self-flagellating. On one occasion Dr. Guyer argued for retention of the *Bulletin's* detailed reports from outlying hospitals. He laughingly observed that Bend doctors like to know who is going out of town for treatment. On another occasion, Ford dealer Gordon Robberson contributed to Chandler's skepticism of police statistics when he remarked that his car lot was burglarized at least five nights a week. "I've quit reporting these thefts. The police have no clues and can do nothing, but when they record the crime, up go my insurance rates."

The constituencies that loomed behind all the members were even more apparent in Redwood City, a populous, fragmented community where council members were conscious of the demographic reasons for their membership. For example, painters' union representative Tim Kelly had no more than recommended a labor column for the *Tribune* than teacher Byron Skinner plumped for an educator-of-the-week feature, and businessman Walt Small urged a know-your-merchant series. Suddenly realizing the extent of their lobbying, all three grinned sheepishly.

Mrs. Aldene Smith, a retired teacher, after commenting on the *Tribune's* teen section, turned to Greg Herman, the high school student member. "I know that lots of mothers and grandmothers think the section is just great, but how do you students feel about it?" Publisher Spangler was also curious. "Don't hold back," he said, "I'm interested in getting your reactions. What do they say about us on campus?"

"I've heard lots of complaints about Bob McLeod's column in the teen section," Herman reported. "He seems to be preachy, expressing *his* opinions in a section that is supposed to be for young people. He attacks our major interests—the Beatles, for example. He's way off when he talks about music. He writes a lot about the Monkees, which is not a popular group with teen-agers. He's not offensive; he just doesn't know where it's at. On the other hand, we like the *Tribune's* stories on cars and college." He considered the *Tribune's* sports page adequate for teen tastes. Then, pleased at having so many attentive adult ears, he cited a paradox that was apparent to his constituents: "We live in a society that is more interested in sports than scholarship. If you look at our graduation requirements you'll find that we need four years of physical education and only three of English."

Through dialogues such as these—sometimes weighty, often light, and occasionally punctuated by fresh insights—the councils became forums where diverse interests could converse with the press. There were a few jolts for the laymen, as when Mrs. Langmas learned the depth of the *Bulletin's* disdain for the Community Concerts, and when Judge Foley discovered that newspapers frequently tidy up the grammar of newsmakers. "This is a revelation to me," Foley said. "I thought all quotes were sacred, and printed exactly as stated." The Bend council also was startled to learn that not every letter to the editor found its way into print; Chandler rationed two compulsive correspondents to one letter a month.

The newspapermen, too, were occasionally brought up short. As long as the *Tribune* has a special section on business, the members wondered, why can't it have a labor page? "Frankly," editor Schutz answered bleakly, "I've never asked myself that." A bit later, Mrs. Henderson complained about the very idea of a women's page. "People—meaning men—have an inclination to think 'we girls' are interested in something entirely different from what you are interested in, and you want to discriminate by segregating the news." Again Schutz was taken aback. "We've had women's and sports pages for generations. Maybe this is the wrong approach." As the Bend council analyzed accident stories, Judge Foley asked if routine collision stories couldn't be summarized in a "news of record" column. Managing editor Yates scratched his head. "Maybe that *would* be a good place to put those stories. This really never occurred to me."

"We Have to Become Sensitive"

What *really* never occurs to newspapermen, some critics say, is to pay the right kind of attention to minority groups. Nationwide, the number of black journalists is low—small-city papers, in fact, usually have none. And yet with racism a national malaise, small cities need to be as attuned as big cities to minority voices. Although Bend has only one black family, 2000 of Redwood City's 65,000 population are black and its schools enroll 1100 Spanish-surnamed children. If Redwood City's race relations are outwardly quiet, Spangler saw no reason for complacency. "We have to teach ourselves to become sensitive," he told his council. "We're learning, but we need new watchtowers."

The press council provided him a watchtower in black high school teacher Byron Skinner. One of Skinner's first council contributions was advice to the *Tribune* on how to cope with a black woman running for city council who did not wish to be identified by race or have her picture published. Spangler was inclined, as a matter of routine, to run her picture with those of other candidates, but he also wanted to be sensitive to the special needs of minorities. Skinner reassured him: "Negroes should be proud. The woman should be identified." Her picture did appear, and she did not complain.

Less easily accepted by the *Tribune* and the white members of the council were Skinner's observations on the pervasiveness of racism within American society—including Redwood City. He was especially critical of an editorial that appeared following a meeting of Citizens Against Racism, a group formed by Redwood City liberals after the assassination of Martin Luther King. The editorial denounced certain Black Panther Party positions that had been introduced at the meeting. Skinner said the editorial was a product of white thinking:

> What happened was this: The white upper-middle class got together and said they ought to listen to black people and follow what the blacks said. I went to the meeting and this white minister kept saying, "Tell us what you want, tell us what you want, tell us what you want." So a Panther got up and read off ten points—what *he* wanted. When we came back the next week, the whites said this was not what *they* wanted. Now, the *Tribune* editorial only mentioned two of his ten points—letting all black people out of jails and not requiring blacks to serve in Vietnam— and without fully explaining even those two points.
>
> The editorial said, "A realistic assessment of the problem is needed." Well, who's to say which assessment is realistic? If a Black Panther, an individual from the ghetto, does not have a realistic assessment, who does? The only way people who don't live in these areas will ever understand the problem is to take off the glasses they are wearing and look at the problem through another set of lenses. I think the newspaper can be instrumental in making this leap into reality.
>
> Redwood City has the idea that it is in a favorable position and does not have the kinds of problems that exist in East Palo Alto and San Francisco. Well, maybe we'd better get going so we won't have those problems five years from now.

As though trying to demonstrate Skinner's point about white lenses, the members of the council struggled to grasp his meaning. "I just don't understand," Al Hinners blustered. "What gripes me is all this talk about Black Power. What difference does it make? It's not the color that counts. I've lived with black people, worked with them, and some of them are my good friends."

"I know it doesn't make any difference to you, Al," Skinner said gently, "but it makes a difference around the country."

Nor could the other members immediately accept Skinner's offhand remark that bias existed in their highly prized school system. "Inequality in *our* schools?" one member asked.

"Let me explain," Skinner said, holding up a copy of the 1968 report of the Kerner Commission on Civil Disorders. "It's all in this book. But, more specifically, we tested a group of Redwood City students in January for their knowledge of black history, and they didn't know the things that most progressive educators said they should know. And when my realtor was telling a local person that I was a teacher of black culture courses, the gentlemen replied, 'What culture do they have?' Now, *you* can't see these things because you are not black. Whites have to learn that white and black kids are systematically prevented from seeing the true story of America."

Attorney William Keogh probed for a summary and some direction for the *Tribune.* "I'm not entirely clear, Byron, but are you saying that the editorial was a piece of rather bad reporting?"

"I think it reflects a typical white reaction," Skinner said. "I think we all should keep an open ear to radical organizations and see if in fact some of the charges they make aren't true."

"If I interpret you correctly," Keogh said, "you are describing the editorial as a white man's effort to report something that he is constitutionally unable to understand."

"That's right. I'm concerned about creating in Redwood City, and every other city, an atmosphere where the whites are willing to step out of their own ghetto and see whether we really should try some of these things, instead of having a showdown with guns."

In Bend a similar problem that had no racial connotation was faced when Ray Hickman attempted to tell Chandler how hard it was for laboring people to air their views widely. He began: "A lot of people have ideas that they think would benefit the whole community." He stopped, pondered, then sensing that the other members had begun to think about the letters column, continued: "They don't have the time—don't feel that they have the know-how to sit down and write a good letter to the editor. I wonder if maybe a suggestion column on the editorial page—I wonder if people could just send in a short suggestion and then maybe the newspaper could take it and do something about it."

His fellow members were momentarily baffled, but Chandler began to understand. He explained the idea of "action lines"—problem-solving columns through which a newspaper serves as an ombudsman between troubled readers and bureaucracy. I added that some action lines have space for one-paragraph statements of opinion from readers. Hickman looked relieved, but not entirely satisfied. He was trying to help everyone understand that working-class people with little education suffered a kind of double jeopardy—they were intimidated by the task of writing and by the chance that a forceful editor would publicly scoff at their efforts—and yet they felt their ideas were worthy of ventilation. He was telling Chandler that the *Bulletin* was more than arm's length away from this kind of reader, who was in effect isolated from the rest of the community. Chandler understood.

Even a seemingly outrageous suggestion may have some value for the perceptive publisher. When the Bend council discussed ways of gaining readership for important but unspectacular stories on budgets of public agencies, member Hollern lightly observed, "Why don't you just run the story on the front page—only so big—and leave all the rest of the page blank? That would be one way of saying the story is really important." The other members guffawed, but Chandler remained silent and thoughtful. "We think we have tried every possible way to present such stories—using narrative form, tabular form, the example of a typical taxpayer, diagrams, pictures, pie charts, bar charts, and a second front page. It's pretty discouraging after an election to have people say they didn't read anything about it. You're right—we must do something new." Hollern's unusual suggestion stimulated Chandler to review many devices for emphasizing a story, and he was reminded how important tax stories are within his community.

Advice Is There for the Taking

The councils often seemed to be communicating more than words. This also appeared to be the case when the Bend council demonstrated its ignorance of juvenile court procedure. Afterward Chandler reflected on the members' surprising naïveté and concluded that it was high time to write an explanatory editorial on juvenile justice in Oregon.

Sometimes the newspapermen were disappointed to find little interest in long-established sections of the paper, but even then there were important clues for the publishers. The *Tribune's* executives wanted the council's views on the women's section, but found a lack of enthusiasm, even among the female council members. Dr. Rivers had asked, with a certain degree of male indulgence, not if the women liked the section, but how much they liked it. Mrs. Henderson responded more as a political activist, which she is, than as a housewife, which she also is. "Here's my basic frustration: If I'm going to read about Portola Valley or Woodside, I'd be more interested in knowing what their planning commission is doing than what trip somebody is taking."

"Well now," Spangler said, "what do you think about the Maribeth column?" This is a column of sprightly comments about the excursions of suburban socialities.

"I don't read it," Mrs. Henderson said.

"I don't like it," Mrs. Smith said.

"I scan it quickly to see if I recognize any names," Mrs. Ruby Phillips said. "Otherwise I skip it." Spangler and Schutz looked wounded. "I'm sorry," she added.

The males were completely in the dark. "What does she [Maribeth] write about, anyhow?" Kelly asked.

"The doings of Peninsula people, for the most part," said Schutz glumly.

"Oh," said Kelly.

The moderator attempted to salvage something for the *Tribune*. "Don't you ladies have friends who read this column?"

"I've never heard them comment on it," Mrs. Smith said. "I doubt it's their life blood."

Nor did the women read the bridge column. Mrs. Henderson said she preferred the San Francisco *Chronicle's* bridge expert. Mrs. Phillips said she read a column called "Polly's Pointers" only when there was nothing else of interest in the paper. The others didn't read it at all. What the women agreed they wanted was local general news. "We're interested in women's news not because we're women but because we're interested in *news*," Mrs. Smith said.

The *Tribune* had offered a women's section for many years, and it was depressing to Spangler and Schutz to find so little interest in it among the ladies of the council. The *Tribune* men, of course, could write off the three women as eccentrics among their thousands of readers. Still, as Schutz noted, perhaps newspapermen ought to raise a few questions about the long-established habit of sectioning.

Certainly the women's views were enlightening to one of their fellow members, Walter Small, who was in charge of advertising for his J. C. Penney store.

"Where would you be more likely to notice one of our ads," Small asked, "on the women's page or on page three or five?"

"Dare I answer?" Mrs. Phillips said with a sidelong glance at the publisher. "I would probably see it more often if it were in another section. If there's any part I don't get around to reading, it's the women's." The other women agreed. Mrs. Henderson added a pet peeve: "The underwear ads are always on the women's page, just as if women never read another part of the paper. If you have a good ad, put it anywhere."

Small looked up from the notes he had been taking. "Maybe we advertisers have had some screwy notions about where we should put our ads. Come to think of it, men probably buy more women's sleepwear than women do, especially before some of the holidays. I'll just bet that our Mother's Day ads will be more effective on the sports pages. I may go ahead and put them there—really." Later, in fact, his Penney store began doing just that.

Some Serendipity

Like the fabled princes of Serendip, the council members made many agreeable and unexpected discoveries, not the least of which were revelations about their own communities. In the Bend council, Hickman expressed a wish that common laborers could meet with high school students on the verge of dropping out so that the students could "learn how tough it is to make a living without an education." Judge Foley responded immediately: "You've just been recruited into Operation Total Involvement." This was a new organization headed by Foley which sought to bring Bend youth into the mainstream of community life. Not all the council members had heard of it, and Hickman was pleased to join.

The side effect most apparent to the members was their own learning experiences. Mrs. Ruth Burleigh had a typical reflection: "I can't help but think this experience has taught me an enormous amount about newspapers." They also learned something about, among other things, the extent of poverty in their communities, the depths of racial feelings, the alienation of students, the merchandising problems of businessmen, the effects of business consolidations, the frustrations of publicity-seekers, the strategies of politicians, the reading habits of housewives, and even the effects of computers on insurance rates.

But serendipity was not all on the side of the members. The two publishers entered the experience with some fear of criticism and attacks. Often they found support. If one council member saw something to assail, another usually rose to the newspaper's defense. When Dr. Guyer complained that Chandler was not fully receptive to outside ideas, Judge Foley replied, "If you've been around a newspaper very much you realize that many problems are the facts of life that must be lived with, just as there are some things in the medical business that you might like to do something about but can't. We've brought up many things about which Mr. Chandler has said, 'Well, we can't do this,' and he has given good and valid reasons. But there are several areas, I'm sure, where there have been good discussions and he has got quite a bit out of it—and these things have been of interest even to you."

Occasionally a member defended the newspaper outside of the council meetings. In Redwood City, Hinners made three progress reports on his council participation to his union local and to the county labor council. When several union men buttonholed him about their gripes with the *Tribune*, Hinners was able to explain *Tribune* practices. The support in and out of the council did not go unappreciated. Spangler remarked, "During our period with the press council we went through some rather traumatic experiences, and it was refreshing to find understanding and support for our position, a degree of forgiveness for our sins, and relatively few uncompromised opinion positions at the end of the experiment." He was thinking particularly of the *Tribune's* policy of disclosing the names of juveniles arrested for felonies, which had come under severe attack through letters and telephone calls. Feeling ran high in his council, too, but the members were divided—and agreeable to hearing opposing views. After careful consideration, the *Tribune* did change its policy in the direction of less disclosure, thanks in part to the council's deliberations.

Each of the eighteen members of the two councils was surveyed before and after the experience for his opinions of the newspaper. A modified version of the Brinton-Bush-Newell[2] test of attitudes toward newspapers revealed that only three of the members did not change their opinions one way or another, five expressed a lower opinion of their newspapers, and ten exhibited a higher opinion at the end of the period.

The general public also seemed to think more highly of the newspaper if it knew the paper was being counseled, according to the results of two surveys conducted in Bend.[3] One of the devices used to generate topics for council discussion—as well as to measure an aspect of newspaper quality—was a survey of every person who had been significantly mentioned in local news stories during a selected period. Each person was mailed a clipping of the story mentioning him with a questionnaire that asked if the story was accurate. The questionnaire also asked the respondent for his opinion of the newspaper. To determine whether knowledge of the press council made any difference in public opinion, the questionnaires were mailed under alternate cover letters, one that briefly mentioned the council and one that did not. Thus, half of the persons surveyed were sure to have heard of the council; the other half might not have heard.

Two accuracy surveys were administered. Both times the average opinion of the newspaper was higher for those respondents who knew of the council—a finding that indicates some public-relations value in press councils. It might be argued that those who received the council cover letter may have inflated their opinions out of fear that word would get back to the publisher, but the fact that response rates were slightly higher to the council cover letter suggests no reticence.

Chandler was pleased to hear these findings, but hardly over-whelmed. As a hard-nosed journalist he was ambivalent, to say the least, toward public relations (at one time in his career in Bend he had been hanged in effigy, to his vast unconcern). That his council had public-relations value for the *Bulletin* was unimportant to him. He was more interested in the members' comments and criticisms.

Somebody's Watching

When George Murray, a director of Associated Newspapers Ltd., completed four years as chairman of the British Press Council in 1963,[4] he remarked that if anyone asked what had been the council's greatest achievement, he would reply, "We survived."

It may have been a greater achievement for the Bend and

Redwood City councils to survive to the ends of their prescribed terms. Whereas a statutory council receives governmental resuscitation, voluntary councils are free to fail at any time. The newspaper's representatives are no more required to attend than to accede to the voluntary council's wishes. Yet only illness or long-standing commitments ever prevented the two West Coast publishers from attending, and more than once they gave up other obligations in order to participate. The members also attended regularly, and at the end of the experience only one of the eighteen said he would not care to serve again if asked. Both publishers said they contemplated a continuation of their councils. (Chandler did reconstitute his council with a local attorney as moderator. Spangler, who was on the verge of retirement, left the question to his successor.)

Chandler felt his council's mere presence was salutary: "My staff knew someone else was now watching them, and that I was getting a better idea of how the public was regarding their work."

In Spangler's view, "A valuable by-product is a sense of responsibility one enjoys when he knows a problem cannot merely be swept into a newspaper wastebasket if a press council is sitting nearby to ask questions about the ultimate disposition of the problem."

Superficially, there seems to be a little connection between the many modest questions posed by the press council members and the major issues of press performance raised by the nation's leading press critics. Few seem to attack "the deeply rooted traditions and conventions that no longer serve a viable journalism," to borrow Ralph D. Casey's words.[5] Yet these groups of inexpert volunteers were able to work at least a few useful changes in an institution not famous for its ability to change. According to Carl Lindstrom, "Journalism (the recorder of change) has feared change, as if it meant death."[6]

Actually, however, seemingly innocuous questions can run quite deep. A simple query as to why a newspaper puts a length restriction on letters to the editor is only a half-step away from the deep and controversial issue of the public's right of access to print. The councils did indeed raise major issues, but in their own fashion—not under heraldic banners such as "The Role of the Press vis-à-vis the Subculture of Anomic Youth." More often, deep issues were posed through homely inquiries like "How in hell can the newspaper get through to the kids in our town?"

Notes

[1] Lewis Donohew, "Publishers and Their 'Influence' Groups," *Journalism Quarterly*, Winter 1965, pp. 112-13.

[2] James E. Brinton, Chilton R. Bush, and Thomas M. Newell, *The Newspaper and Its Public* (Stanford, Calif.: Institute for Communication Research, 1958).

[3] William B. Blankenburg, "News Accuracy: Some Findings on the Meaning of Errors," *The Journal of Communication*, December 1970, pp. 375-86;

[4] A leading study of the British Press Council is H. Phillip Levy, *The Press Council: History, Procedure and Cases* (New York: St. Martin's Press, 1967).

[5] Ralph D. Casey (ed.), *The Press in Perspective* (Baton Rouge, La.: Louisiana State University Press, 1963), p. xvii.

[6] Carl E. Lindstrom, *The Fading American Newspaper* (Garden City, N.Y.: Doubleday, 1960), p. 17.

CHAPTER FOUR

A Question of Leadership

by KENNETH STARCK

> If I were the editor, I think I would spend a
> lot more time crusading. I would challenge
> the community on some of the big issues.
> Through the front page and through the
> editorial page. Some things need to be said
> that aren't being said.
>
> —David McMeekin Conn,
> Sparta press council member

From the days of Howe Vernon Morgan to those of his son William
Howe Morgan, the Sparta, Illinois, *News-Plaindealer* has made some
obvious changes. Recipient of many awards for distinguished community journalism, the paper is now housed in a $200,000 plant
dedicated in 1967.

The publisher's weekly column, which was begun by Howe
Morgan during the Depression to build community morale when "all of
us needed it," is "The Week With Bill" instead of "And Howe." The
high quality of the offset printing and photographic reproduction are
also obvious—and different.

But the most important changes may be neither obvious nor
superficial. Perhaps in earlier days the challenges facing the residents of
this small community were easier to identify and cope with through a
newspaper. Bombarded by other media much as the residents of the
metropolitan centers are, perhaps the 3452 Spartans need not rely as
heavily on the weekly *News-Plaindealer* as they did when Howe Morgan
was editor. In any case, consider these views of members of the Sparta
Community Press Council:

"This is not to take away from Bill," one said, "but I do think his
father took stronger stands on issues."

"His [Bill's] editorials are usually for motherhood, baseball, and so forth," added another, a local school official. "They seem to be written from the standpoint of 'this is the thing to do.' "

"Indeed," commented an attorney on the council, "it does seem that the editorials in the *News-Plaindealer* take a consistently safe position. Bill's dad took a position we often didn't go along with, but made us think."

Inadvertently, perhaps, the council members had touched on three concepts that were to serve as intermittent flares setting off the council discussions that took place in Sparta: press function, press responsibility, press leadership. Most of the time it seemed impossible to separate one from another.

"Tremendous Responsibility"

Howe Vernon Morgan, who in 1921 combined two weeklies, the *News* and the *Plaindealer,* was widely acclaimed for trying to improve Sparta and for fighting corruption in state government.[1] His candid editorials and columns were often quoted.

In 1929 he helped organize a Chamber of Commerce for Sparta with: "The time is ripe to come to our senses and bind all professional men in an active club for the advancement of the best interests of the town." His weekly columns frequently reflected his newspapering philosophy:

I feel that country editors have a tremendous responsibility. They speak each week to an audience which would cause any preacher or small town orator to have stage fright. Take me, for instance. This paper is read each week by more than 4,000 families. If there were only three readers in each family, that means 12,000 people in my audience. Perhaps it's natural that a few out of that number won't like what I say and will tell me about it. Guess I'm lucky to be alive.

Concerning the newspaper's role in the community, he wrote:

A wide-awake newspaper can make a thriving community out of a country crossroads and the editor who faces that fact and acts accordingly surely has an opportunity.

Located in the Kaskaskia and Mississippi valleys, Sparta did emerge as a prosperous community with a diversified economic base that includes coal mining, railroad shops, agriculture, and a publishing house that produces so many magazines—more than 1,250,000 copies of comic books alone every day—that the city refers to itself as the "magazine capital of the world." Sparta is also headquarters for various Randolph County and district offices and is a trade and market center for the area. The newspaper has prospered with the area and now has a circulation of about 5500.

On June 1, 1945, Howe Morgan announced to readers of his column that his son would be given a variety of jobs around the newspaper that summer. "I hope he likes it," he wrote. "Otherwise I'll probably be working hard the rest of my life."

Six years later, young Bill Morgan was graduated from the University of Illinois School of Journalism and became acting editor, advertising manager, and business manager of the *News-Plaindealer*. When his father died in 1966 Bill became editor and publisher.

Crusades? Yes, No

Bill Morgan agreed in 1968 to cooperate with a press council whose purpose was to serve as a channel for informational exchange between the newspaper and a fairly representative segment of its audience. But it was not long before council members began trying to determine for themselves what role the newspaper played—or was supposed to play—in the community. What task was the *News-Plain-dealer* performing? Should it be an active leader in the community? Indeed, the answers may be peculiar to weeklies, which often have different functions in the small communities that nurture them than do

Dr. Starck is Associate Professor in the College of Journalism at the University of South Carolina. He was Assistant Professor in the Southern Illinois University School of Journalism when he served as field director of the Southern Illinois press councils. Dr. Starck was moderator for all meetings of the two councils in Sparta and Cairo.

papers in larger towns.[2] The question of Morgan's weekly editorials came up at an early session.

Bill Morgan, who is not verbose, answered the council's charge: "We could be more crusading, but it's kind of out of style." Shortly afterward, he wrote an editorial holding:

> One of the criticisms which has been repeatedly mentioned at meetings of the press council is the need for more frequent "crusading" editorials. We agree, and only regret that most weeks time does not permit the research which must precede the writing of regular "old-fashioned" crusading editorials. Since an editorial is an expression of the author's opinion, the author must have an ample knowledge of his subject in order to draw an intelligent conclusion.

Morgan, a former president of the Illinois Press Association, is fully aware of the shadow cast by his father. And if it is true that long-tenured editors often establish themselves as spokesmen for the public and are instrumental in developing public opinion,[3] then the converse may also hold: a comparatively new editor must pass through a period of confidence-building before gaining public acceptance. It is also true, of course, that experience enables an editor to become more informed about his community's needs.

"Bill seems to be evading the question of a newspaper's leadership role in the community," remarked the attorney. "Isn't one of the chief responsibilities of a newspaper to have a crusading spirit?"

"Because of this lack of a crusading spirit," added another councilman, "the newspaper seems to lack community involvement. There seems to be no place, no group, where someone can go and get something worthwhile done in this town. Perhaps there should be another organization composed of representatives of all other organizations which could serve as a leadership group."

The paper could and should provide leadership, Morgan agreed. He said it must also build the community: "The better the community, the better the newspaper. And when some hands need slapping, then the newspaper must do so." Sharing his thoughts not only with council members but with readers of his editorial page, he wrote that most editorials have one of three purposes—to inform, interpret, or amuse. He added:

They express our attitudes on various questions of the day. These editorials express our opinions. We do not expect agreement on all points, but we do hope to get our readers to think for themselves so they may compare ideas with those presented in an editorial. Through stimulating thought, it is our hope to stimulate progress for our area.

"We don't always have the time necessary to thoroughly research some topics," Bill Morgan told the council. "But we do consider the editorials a key part of our newspaper." Each issue carries three or four editorials set in large type and headed *This Is Our Humble Opinion.* Writing them is the chief reason the publisher's work week far exceeds the usual 40 to 44 hours.

Council members reported they read the editorials in the *News-Plaindealer*, but sometimes they thought the publisher should have treated different subjects. One session generated a sharp discussion of the lack of editorial comment on the assassination of Martin Luther King, Jr.

"I heard some criticism," began one of the black council members, a retired school teacher, "over the failure of the *News-Plaindealer* to carry an article, say an editorial, about the assassination of Martin Luther King."

"This was a national news event," countered another council member, "and it was covered by the daily media. I wonder what place this would have in a weekly newspaper. What enlightenment could we have gotten out of it?"

About 10 percent of Sparta's 3452 residents are black, and several members said they were surprised at the number of their acquaintances who felt the newspaper should have commented editorially on the death of the Negro leader.

Morgan responded, "I didn't even think about it. It fell out of the realm of local news. And it's not our policy to cover or comment upon nonlocal news events. But many people spoke to me about it; I had no idea the feeling was so strong locally."

Then he told council members to check the next edition of the *News-Plaindealer*. The lead editorial was headlined *A Deeply Felt Loss:*

Times are changing and it is important that the local press keep up with the times. We have, for many years, operated this newspaper on the theory that our readers expect from us news coverage and editorial comment on local events. . . .

When President Kennedy was assassinated, it was not mentioned in the News-Plaindealer. Not since the advent of radio and same-day distribution of daily newspapers in rural communities has the weekly press in general given space to national news.

However, had we realized how deeply the assassination of Dr. King was felt in our community, and what a very personal loss this was to many of our friends, we would most certainly have expressed concern and sorrow. His murder was a tragedy. His death was a great loss to the peaceful solution of the great civil rights issue.

Another editorial topic that evoked council concern was political endorsements and partisan political issues in general. Most council members seemed to oppose editorials dealing directly with politics. The reason may have been, as one councilman put it, that editorial opinion in a community weekly tends to be construed as reflecting community opinion. Or as another councilman said, editorial endorsement of candidates simply does not carry much weight because it is generally believed that citizens are in as good a position as the editor-publisher to judge the qualifications of political candidates.

In this setting, the publisher announced to the council that for the first time in twenty years the newspaper would endorse a political candidate, Paul Simon, for lieutenant-governor of Illinois. There may or may not have been a connection, but in that November election, Simon, who was elected to the office, polled 7349 votes in Randolph County as compared to his opponent's 6611.

Defining Function

In addition to examining the leadership role of newspapers, the press council sought to define the functions of the community newspaper.

Council members brought to the task a diverse set of ideas and experiences. Of the sixteen originally selected to represent a cross section of the community, twelve remained active throughout the press council experience. They were: a housewife who was president of the Sparta Human Relations Council, a district telephone company manager, an attorney, a retired school teacher, a banker, a high school principal, an executive of a large printing company, an agricultural extension adviser, a housewife active in numerous community projects, a businessman, a commercial photographer, and a dentist. Council membership included three blacks, although one was not active.

Publisher Morgan attended the monthly meetings regularly. Early in its life, the council decided—and Morgan agreed—that because the publisher was on a first-name basis with most of the members and his presence might inhibit criticism, he should attend only the second half of each meeting.

The council generally agreed that the community newspaper has three functions: (1) to report local news, (2) to serve as a vehicle for advertising, and (3) to promote community leadership.

There were sharp differences of opinion about the most effective means of implementing the local coverage and leadership functions. And interpreting these tasks sparked lively discussions.

"Is the newspaper," asked the school principal, "ever justified in covering up dissension in a community? Or, to rephrase it, should the newspaper print facts as they are or should it cover up facts because it may be bad for the town?"

"The newspaper," said the attorney, "has a tremendous responsibility to print the facts."

Morgan responded that "getting the facts is often very difficult." The problem was emphasized for most council members when they listened to a young couple from North Carolina describe their difficulties in Sparta as workers of VISTA (Volunteers In Service To America). They had been invited to appear before the council at the request of a member who felt the *News-Plaindealer* had not been adequately covering VISTA. What the couple told the members about their apparently prosperous community surprised most of them. The VISTA workers said that a number of residents of Sparta could at best be described as on the fringe of society—people suffering from hunger, alcoholism, and lack of adequate medical care. Does the paper have a responsibility to them?

The paper certainly has a responsibility for airing community problems, Morgan told the council. As for covering the activities of the VISTA workers, he said the paper had been receiving excellent cooperation from the North Carolina couple. Asked about a request by the VISTA workers that they write a regular column on VISTA projects, the publisher said he "approached this with fear and trembling. As an editor, you have to have control of everything that goes into the newspaper; otherwise, it can get out of hand."

When a council member spoke against making space available to any group for fear the group might make personal attacks on individuals or even the community, Morgan answered that a publisher is legally responsible for the contents of the entire paper.

Council members tended to agree that a paper does not have an obligation to instigate efforts to provide direct assistance to needy citizens. Instead, the paper perhaps should serve as a channel through which others, including organized groups, could work to offer direct aid.

"After all," asked one member, "is the newspaper's job to make the news or to report the news?"

Another underscored the point: "The newspaper's main function here should be to make people aware."

One black council member, objecting to the paper's failure to "go out and look for the news," complained that too little attention had been given to a project through which, with the cooperation of several groups including the VISTA workers, water lines had been extended to an economically poor area on the outskirts of Sparta. Further, she charged, the paper had not even carried a story about the dedication of the project, even though the Sparta mayor was to speak at the ceremony.

Morgan asserted that he believed the project had been covered adequately, although the dedication had been omitted through an oversight. "We could use another full-time reporter," the publisher told the council, "but it's a matter of economics." For conveying news to the newspaper, he mentioned at another time, "We have to depend on others more than we'd like to."

One councilman held that lack of personnel for gathering information firsthand is particularly dangerous in the case of controversial stories. One such story investigated racial tension among students of Sparta high school. Local NAACP officials apparently felt black students were not wholly integrated into school activities, while school officials maintained that there was no discrimination.

"It would be advisable," said another council member, "for the newspaper in a case like this to be able to assign a man to handle the story—to check all the angles in it."

Because of the shortage of personnel, Morgan told the council, it was not ordinarily possible to staff school board meetings as well as meetings of some other agencies. Information concerning school board actions came from the minutes and from school officials. Press council members also complained about inadequate coverage of city council meetings. The publisher explained that lengthy meetings were impossible to cover entirely, and, consequently, the city clerk was interviewed the day after each meeting to supplement coverage. But the press council was so concerned over coverage of city council proceedings that the publisher soon arranged to cover the entire meeting.

One woman press council member observed, "Sometimes it seems as though the *News-Plaindealer* does not follow up stories from one issue to the next. And sometimes the information is incomplete."

"We try to follow up every story that needs following up," Morgan replied. "And sometimes lack of information isn't our fault. For example," he nodded toward the attorney, "when a civil suit is settled out of court, the attorneys usually won't give us any details."

"Some of the stories I've submitted, as well as stories others have turned in, frequently are changed," the woman persisted. "And sometimes parts are left out."

"I reserve the right to edit or rewrite anything that goes into the newspaper," Morgan said.

Another member remarked at one session that some news appears "old and stale" by the time it appears in the *News-Plaindealer*.

Morgan responded that the paper tries to be "on top of the news," notably by keeping a detailed ledger of community activities. The biggest problem, he said, is that many readers expect the editor somehow to know about all newsworthy happenings but make no effort to inform him about events. If the public expects a wide range of information, he said, then the public must cooperate.

"Of course," he commented with a smile, "we do have some readers like one woman who told me she always knows what's in the *News-Plaindealer*. 'Why do you read it then?' I asked. 'Well,' she said, 'I just want to know if you people over at the newspaper found out too.' "

Council Noses for News

Council members often suggested stories and editorials. One recommended that the paper carry more news about local men in the armed services. "We can do it if people let us know about the news," replied Morgan. The councilman also asked for more news from nearby communities experiencing problems similar to those of Sparta, and the need for reviving the county planning commission. An editorial several weeks later presented the case for reactivating the commission, concluding: "Until this is done, all the money, the effort and the hopes that were put into the organization are wasted and the county is without a workable plan for the future."

Members also suggested grouping movie advertisements rather than scattering them throughout the several sections of the newspaper, printing a page-one index to the contents of each issue, grouping related stories, reducing the number of stories continued from page one, and adding a weekly feature or column about teenagers. The publisher adopted some of the suggestions and explained why it was impossible to do so with others.

"Perhaps English classes in the school district could provide stories or material for a feature appealing to young people," a member suggested.

"That would be fine," agreed Morgan, "but the main problem is getting copy from the various groups."

Some news tips and story ideas originated with readers who had channeled their comments to individual council members. The council actively encouraged citizen assessment of the paper, and Morgan wrote an editorial expressing members' sentiments. In addition to explaining the purpose of the council and listing the members' names, the editorial stated:

> Members of the press council would benefit and would appreciate comments from other members of the community. Anyone having suggestions as to how the News-Plaindealer can better serve its community, or having constructive criticism to offer is asked to talk with a member of the press council.

"Community Conscience"

Council members constantly reverted in their discussion to lack of leadership—from the newspaper as well as from any other agency in the community. More than any other topic, this was to emerge and reemerge as the thematic backdrop to the Sparta press council discussions. It came up in connection with the search for the purpose or function of the *News-Plaindealer* in Sparta. The council member who seemed to enunciate the consensus most accurately was the attorney.

"The freedom of the press," he said, "seems to suggest that a newspaper should also be a conscience of the community. We tend to avoid problems which do not affect us directly. A newspaper—if it is a responsible paper and if it has a function—can nip at everyone's conscience once in a while. Needling is more effective than dictating."

It came up again in connection with the responsibility of the *News-Plaindealer* in Sparta. "What we need is some centralized location for working with the city's problems. Newspapers are such a place. The newspaper must help."

And again, when the discussion turned to a hypothetical question of what each council member would do if he were editor:

"I think I would spend a lot more time crusading. I would challenge the community on some of the big issues. This is the one area weekly newspapers can play an important role in. Through the front page and through the editorial page, I could hit these things. There is much news that isn't astonishing. Some things need to be said that aren't being said."

No Love—or Malice

Function. Responsibility. Leadership. During the first nine meetings, the three concepts sporadically converged and separated. And when the changing patterns finally came into focus at the end of the regular press council period, what was shown? More specifically, what had occurred—in the minds of the press council members and the editor-publisher, and in the pages of the newspaper and among its readers—as a result of the press council experience?

One council member may have aptly summarized the general reaction with: "I'd do it all over again—but I'm not sure what we accomplished." In fact, immediately after the experiment the council did reorganize on a permanent basis, agreeing to expand membership to include high school youth, setting terms of members at three years, scheduling quarterly meetings and adopting this statement of purpose:

The purpose of the Sparta Press Council is to function as an intermediary between the Sparta *News-Plaindealer* and the Sparta community in an effort to promote understanding between the newspaper and its audience.

The Press Council, as an advisory body, will:

1. Evaluate performance of the Sparta *News-Plaindealer;*

2. Encourage and consider communiques, including suggestions, criticism, and comments, from readers of the Sparta *News-Plaindealer*; and

3. Discuss issues pertinent to the Sparta *News-Plaindealer* and the Sparta community.[4]

As for accomplishments:

"We put Bill on his toes," commented a councilman.

Another added, "It made *us* think about some things we didn't think about before."

Said the black councilwoman, "The editor is more open-minded and more fair-minded than before the press council was established."

One result of the press council was that members seemed to become more critical of their newspaper. A series of tests conducted at each meeting indicated the council as a group did not significantly alter its evaluation of the newspaper. However, one member did rate the newspaper significantly higher at the end of the experiment than at the beginning, and over the same period two members rated the newspaper significantly lower.[5]

Was the paper fulfilling its function? No consensus emerged to establish bounds of responsibility or criteria for exercising leadership. But council members seemed to gain a better understanding of the issues, not to mention the difficulties in publishing. The publisher admitted that he had become somewhat complacent.

"I've enjoyed the press council," commented the school official. "It's made us more critical. And I think we understand some of Bill's problems better."

"The surprising thing," said the attorney, reflecting on the reluctance of other council members to ask for dramatic changes, "was that people don't particularly want the newspaper to make great changes."

Several members felt the council should have received more publicity in order to attract comments and criticisms from other citizens. The *News-Plaindealer* carried several stories and editorials about the work of the press council. Three months after the first council meeting, Morgan had editorialized:

Here in Sparta something unique is happening. A press council has been formed and has been functioning for several months. We are delighted with the press council and feel we have already learned a great deal.

Nonetheless, a survey following the ninth meeting indicated that only a small percentage of readers sampled were familiar with the work of the press council. One member suggested that the newspaper periodically publish a list of the members to remind readers that they could take issues involving the newspaper before the press council.

The publisher placed high value on the council. After hearing the first questions posed by members, he mused, "We've been putting out a newspaper for so long that sometimes we've forgotten why we do certain things." Later, he told the council, "The biggest thing the press council has done for me is to make me more conscious of what people look for and notice in a newspaper. A good many things have surprised me. And I could explain to others some of my own problems."

Morgan's most cogent assessment of the press council experience was directed to his readers in an editorial:

> The monthly meetings of this council have been extremely rewarding for us. We feel we have gained considerable understanding of what our readers expect of us. We have received constructive criticism in a number of fields. These meetings have not been "love fests" nor have they been malicious. The press council members have asked many questions, given their opinions on many questions and have offered ideas from which we feel we have benefited.

He supported the decision to establish the council permanently; however, after several meetings the council dissolved. The reason: As I dropped out of the picture as moderator, there was no one to take this role, and Bill Morgan thought it improper to conduct the press council himself.

The Reader's View

There was one other attempt to gauge the effects of the press council in Sparta. It consisted of a two-part survey of audience attitudes utilizing the Brinton-Bush-Newell test. The questionnaire was administered twice to a sample of 221 Sparta residents—first before the council was organized, then after the ninth meeting. A total of 142 before-and-after interviews were completed.[6] Although one must be extremely careful in suggesting a causal relationship between the activity of the press council and audience attitudes, the results on three dimensions gave the newspaper more favorable ratings after the press council experience than before. These were: confidence in leadership in political issues and candidates, political and economic fairness, and independence from pressure. On one of the thirteen dimensions, adequacy of news content, there was noticeably more disfavor after the press council experience than before. Differences for the rest of the attitude dimensions were barely perceptible. Among the attitude dimensions in which the difference was appreciable, only one was statistically significant: confidence in leadership in political issues and candidates.[7] Council members, of course, had criticized the *News-Plain-dealer* for its failure to speak out forcefully in its editorials. A further analysis of survey results, however, showed that those readers who could recall the existence of the council did not change their attitude toward the newspaper on this dimension.[8] Informally, council members said they felt the newspaper had become more vigorous editorially during the period under study. As for the publisher, he was at a loss to explain the sole significant finding.

The experience in Sparta suggests that a press council, even in a community where interpersonal relationships tend to be closely drawn, can promote greater understanding between an editor-publisher and his readers. The publisher becomes more attuned to the needs and wishes of his readers. The council members begin to appreciate some of the problems of publishing a newspaper and develop a better understanding of its role. In addition, the Sparta experience suggests that if a newspaper is to function as a vital cog in the community, it must have the cooperation, understanding, and respect of its readers.

One other point is important. Findings of social scientists suggest the community press frequently tends to protect community institutions rather than report the negative aspects.[9] In Sparta council members argued for the newspaper to lead in dealing with—even crusading about—community problems. In this community at least, it seems there was a difference in the editor's perception of his newspaper's role and his readers' perception of it. The press council helped reduce this distance.

Notes

[1] Much of the information about the career of Howe Morgan is taken from Thomas Robert Gray, Jr., "Howe Vernon Morgan, Country Editor," unpublished A.M. thesis, Southern Illinois University, 1964.

[2] Clarice N. Olien, George A. Donohue, and Phillip J. Tichenor, "The Community Editor's Power and the Reporting of Conflict," *Journalism Quarterly*, Summer 1968, p. 244.

[3] William V. D'Antonio, William H. Form, Charles P. Loomis, and Eugene C. Erickson, "Institutional and Occupational Representations in Eleven Community Influence Systems," *American Sociological Review*, June 1961, p. 445.

[4] Kenneth Starck, "Concerning Press Councils . . . Anatomy of a Press Council," *Grassroots Editor*, May-June 1970, pp. 18-22.

[5] L. Erwin Atwood and Kenneth Starck, "Evaluating the Community Press Council," paper presented at annual convention of the Association for Education in Journalism, American University, Washington, D.C., August 1970.

[6] Howard R. Long and Kenneth Starck, "Pilot Demonstration on Developing Community Press Councils in Southern Illinois," report prepared for Mellett Fund for a Free and Responsible Press, October 1968.

[7] On a scale of 5 for "best" and 1 for "worst" score for the newspaper, the before-after means for the attitude dimension were 2.91 and 3.17 ($t = 3.91$, $p < .001$, $df = 120$).

[8] Atwood and Starck, *op. cit.*

[9] Olien, Donohue, and Tichenor, *op. cit.*, p. 252.

CHAPTER FIVE

Crisis in Cairo

by KENNETH STARCK

[Racism in Cairo] is complex and dynamic, but the following factors are involved from the white population's point of view: feelings of racial superiority, a guilt complex, fear of miscegenation and fear of a successful economic, social, political, and legal revolt.

—Albert Shafter, sociologist

On a hot, sunny day in early April 1842, a steamboat churned up the Mississippi River toward the point where the yellow Mississippi absorbs the brown waters of the Ohio River. One passenger, who was known for a sharp eye and a sharper pen, was unmoved by the marriage of the two great rivers. He later wrote:

At length, upon the morning of the third day, we arrived at a spot so much more desolate than any we had yet beheld . . . a hot bed of disease, an ugly sepulchre, a grass uncheered by any gleam of promise; a place without one single quality, in earth or air or water to commend it. . . .

It is doubtful that the writer, Charles Dickens, has ever been a literary favorite of Cairo, Illinois. Of all that has been written about this once-thriving, bustling river town, which at one time had more people than Chicago and a seemingly brighter future, nothing has been more widely quoted than the passage from Dickens' *American Notes*, which concludes ". . . such is this dismal Cairo."[1]

Today, many observers would find it hard to fault Dickens. And although the city of Cairo (pronounced CARE-o) cannot be written off so easily, this southernmost Illinois community does represent a socio-economic laboratory which reflects some of the aspirations and most of the adversities of many American communities. It has bright hopes, but they are seeded with a violent history that has yielded a harvest of problems threatening life itself.

To understand the plight of Cairo today, one need only glimpse the city's faded past. From the upheavals of the Civil War to periodic occupation by National Guardsmen today, Cairo has watched physical disruption and beautiful magnolia thrive side by side.

Welcome to Despair, U.S.A.

At the outbreak of the Civil War, both the Confederate and Union armies coveted Cairo for its river location. Union troops arrived first and took possession on April 22, 1861. Confederate troops were just a dozen miles away. More Union troops arrived, and later that year General U.S. Grant established his headquarters.[2] Cairo became a boom town with population climbing in 1865 to more than 8000. More than 2000 were Negroes, many of whom came up from the South and experienced their first "free land."

Following the Civil War and on into the early twentieth century, Cairo enjoyed a steady growth. Always, civic leaders nurtured greater aspirations, which seemed as inevitable as the joining of the rivers. For, as geographers have pointed out, the only confluence of two great rivers where a large city has not evolved is that of the Ohio and Mississippi.[3]

But perhaps the hope was vain. One investigator has suggested that of the three modes of transport important in Cairo's history— water, rail, and highway—the railroad has been most significant. The junction of the waters, he suggests, was misleading; no major city could have developed there because of the lack of high ground where the rivers meet.[4]

The slow, steady population increase continued until 1920, a watershed year for the city. Cairo's population peaked at 15,203. Since then, with the exception of 1940 when the city gained nearly 1000 residents, the population has been dwindling. The 1960 census listed a population of 9348; the 1970 census, 6277.

Nearly 40 percent of Cairo's residents are black. And it is in the area of race relations that Cairo offers a curious, sometimes bewildering picture. The city for years reflected a cosmopolitan atmosphere. "Only in his treatment of the Negro, with passion and prejudice," according to Albert Shafter, a sociologist who studied the city, "does the white citizen of Cairo fail to display his cosmopolitanism."[5]

In the wake of racial outbursts in Cairo, it has become journalistically fashionable to report the city's latest specific incident as part of the larger racial problem. This was the case in 1962 when the focus was on integrating a swimming pool. Blacks demanded admission. Shortly after the state held that the pool should be integrated, the city of Cairo closed it, inflaming an already tense situation. As of this writing, the pool is still closed. In the summer of 1967, violence flared following the mysterious death of a Negro in the city jail. The National Guard restored order after three days of rioting.

Cairo's problems go deeper than race relations. Many find their roots in an economy that has languished for decades—with race offering only a transparent explanation whose prime virtue is that it can be identified. Less obvious, but just as important as the contrast between black and white, are the figures on poverty.

Situated in an area known as "Little Egypt," Cairo is the seat of Alexander County. In population, Alexander ranks 74th among the state's 102 counties. In poverty, it is near the top. For Cairo, in relation to other Illinois cities with a population of 5000 to 10,000, the "poverty index" is just as foreboding. Cairo ranks among the worst in income and education.[6]

"Welcome to Cairo," begins a promotional booklet, "deep in the southland where magnolia vies with the mimosa." The city is farther south than Richmond, Virginia, and nearer to Memphis than to its own state capital of Springfield. Another publication, this one issued by the U.S. Bureau of the Census, reveals that 9.4 percent of the city's residents are unemployed (compared to 4.5 for the state) and that 44.6 percent have incomes under $3000 (compared to 15 percent for the state). Numerous shacks and boarded-up, long-vacated structures along the main thoroughfares and in many sections of town remind the visitor that the crisis in Cairo is not new—but that it is real and grave.

Opening a Channel

Into this setting came the Cairo Community Press Council, which was designed to serve as a channel of communication between the Cairo *Evening Citizen* and its readers. It was a diverse group: a shoe store owner, a housewife who worked for a credit bureau, a physician's wife, a high school teacher, a minister, a businessman, a housewife active in civic organizations, the director of the county housing authority, a social worker, and a woman who was to become the first black since Reconstruction to be elected to office in Cairo. There were five men and five women. Seven were white, three black.

Organizing a press council in Cairo was not easy. Two black leaders—the president of the local NAACP and an official of the Council for Illinois Migrant Workers—could not be invited to serve because of the objections of nearly every white prospect and several of the other blacks. Two blacks and two whites agreed to serve on the council but never appeared for a meeting—and it is not difficult to understand why. The widespread suspicion among Cairo residents toward one another is often intensified when they deal with outsiders. A researcher from Southern Illinois University who tried in 1967 to interview forty-five Cairo residents completed only nineteen interviews. "An air of manifest hostility was evident during the interviewing," he later wrote me in a memo, "and this, combined with other indicators of community conditions such as housing patterns, suggests an unhealthy community life."

Thus, of the fifteen Cairo residents who agreed to serve on the council, ten participated actively throughout the experience.

There was one other member of the council—for a time. He was a white minister who served during much of the life of the council. But one January afternoon an incident involving him emphasized the tension which lies heavily on Cairo. The minister entered his home and found an elderly black man attacking his wife. The minister picked up his youngster's baseball bat and struck the Negro, killing him. An investigation cleared the minister; no charges were brought. He later resigned from the press council on church stationery bearing the slogan, "The Church in the Heart of the City with the City in Its Heart."

Editorial Relevance

An attractive and matronly member of the Cairo press council cleared her voice and, gaining the attention of the other members, began: "We've been talking about this for some time, and I've just got to ask. Who is Don Oakley?"

This name appeared regularly and without identification above *Evening Citizen* editorials. Many of the editorials were well-written, pleasantly digestible—and as relevant to Cairo, Illinois, as they were to Windsor, Colorado, or Waterville, Maine.

"Mr. Oakley is an editorial writer for the NEA—the Newspaper Enterprise Association," replied the paper's editor and general manager, Martin Brown. "His material is syndicated, and his editorials appear in quite a number of newspapers around the country."

"I don't care who Don Oakley is," shot back a council member. "I'd rather see Martin Brown's by-line up there."

Canned material, the member observed, seemed to make the editorial page ineffective. This may be one reason, he went on, why there were so few letters to the editor. Also, he had long wondered why the newspaper no longer printed "a platform—that is, the things the newspaper stands for."

Martin Brown is a large man who is not easily intimidated. A native of Cairo, he had begun his newspaper career as a carrier boy for the same paper he was to serve as editor and general manager. He had left Cairo to earn bachelor's and master's degrees at the University of Minnesota and to work for the *Minneapolis Star* and *Tribune*. About ten years ago, Brown returned to Cairo to join the *Evening Citizen*, which his family owned and had founded as a weekly in 1885, converting it to a daily a decade later. Brown attended press council sessions regularly except for the first three meetings, which were devoted to discussing the major theories underlying press functions and responsibilities.

"Perhaps the newspaper has been lax with editorials," Brown told the council. "My experience with editorials has been rather poor. Simply slapping around people didn't get the job done in the past. When I came back to Cairo to take over the newspaper, the community was down psychologically and economically. And the editorials that were written at that time were very ineffectual. The newspaper's primary objective is to mirror the community. A number of studies have shown that editorials in newspapers are not very well read."

Later, it was pointed out—and acknowledged by Brown—that editorial power is more a result of selective rather than mass readership, with opinion leaders often looking to a newspaper's editorial page for comment and opinion.

"I think the newspaper should provoke comment on meaningful local issues," observed one member, a black housewife. "I read the Chicago *Defender* regularly, and it carries thought-provoking editorials."

At nearly every meeting, members spoke of the need for local editorials to focus attention on and stimulate thinking about community problems. Their concern seemed to go beyond simply publishing an editorial about a local issue. They were groping for a way to awaken community spirit and direct it toward intelligent consideration of problems facing the community. Perhaps the editorial page was such a device.

Not long after this, at the annual Chamber of Commerce dinner, an official of a local manufacturing firm warned against the further hardening of racial attitudes in the city. He urgently appealed for a dialogue that would bring together dissident elements. A few days later, an editorial headlined *Cairo's Mobilization!* appeared in the *Evening Citizen*. It said, in part:

> In times of crisis, the loud voices of radical minority on both sides of the problem are often heard most frequently and above all others. These are the voices that lead a community to the brink of disaster or beyond. They must be stilled, or drowned in a sea of true voices of leadership, wisdom and strength.

"That," one council member said emphatically, "should have been on the front page."

Other members applauded the editorial. In the first secret ballot—a device used three times—members favored the editorial 11-0.

Brown told the council: "We felt that when a man in his position [the business executive] spoke as he did, it was important to the entire community. It was well timed to get the community to sit up and listen." Recalling earlier racial strife in the city, he added: "In 1962 there was literally no communication between the races. The current rise in militancy, particularly as reflected in an arms race, seriously concerns us."

Council members did not believe that editorials alone could cut through the troubled atmosphere. But editorials seemed to be one instrument for arousing public concern.

"The biggest problem," commented a council member, "is getting people to admit there are problems in this town."

"At our PTA meetings," said another, "teachers usually outnumber the parents."

Added another: "Most of us just don't get interested in anything until we're directly involved in it."

Later, members commented on the increased number of locally written editorials in the *Evening Citizen*. One dealt with the challenge facing the board of education. Another commended the job done by the school administration. Another discussed the shortage of physicians in Southern Illinois. Several members suggested topics for editorial comment. Brown soon conceded that editorials could shed light on problems, acknowledging that the council had prompted him to reexamine the function of the editorial page.

Dominant Theme: Race

But a revised editorial policy could not solve Cairo's deep-rooted problem. Race inevitably came up at council meetings. Eventually, a white muttered, "Isn't there anything else we can talk about?"

However, a black member, in words quivering with the emotion of years of frustration, told the council: "We've about decided that in order to let the people know about the Human Relations Commission, we have got to get a newspaper of our own. People just don't know that we're doing anything with the commission. The only thing we can get in are those little announcements."

Earlier, another black member had displayed an article she had clipped from the Decatur, Illinois, *Herald and Review*, in which a Cairo citizen had been interviewed about the Cairo Human Relations Council. "I can't understand why the item could get such fine treatment in another newspaper," she said, "when as far as I know, it hasn't even been noted in the *Evening Citizen.*"

Perhaps emboldened by the absence of Brown, who had been called out of town, the council voted unanimously to send a letter to the editor requesting coverage of the next Human Relations Council meeting. The letter read:

The Press Council last week expressed concern over lack of

coverage of activities of the Human Relations Commission. The council agreed that the public should be informed of the work of the commission. Accordingly, the council voted unanimously to have me [myself, the field director] write you about the June 11 meeting, urging that the meeting be covered. Together with the council, I hope it will be possible for you to make arrangements for coverage of the meeting.

The *Evening Citizen* did not cover the meeting. And when Brown received a report of the press council meeting—a summary was sent to council participants following each session—he responded to the letter as well as to several other criticisms involving errors in stories and failure to cover certain problems in the community. His reaction was immediate and sharp. For a time it seemed that the incident might permanently disrupt the council's functioning. In a memo to me, Brown wrote: "Is the press council doing the job for which it was designed? It seems to me that it is busy in dealing with petty issues. . . . I think that you may realize by now that there is an extreme amount of pettiness in Cairo and this has affected everything anyone attempts to accomplish."

"In reality," he concluded, "this community and its people don't deserve a daily newspaper."

Later he responded directly to the council. The Human Relations Council—not "Commission," he corrected council members—served as an advisory group to the city council and, as such, held no legal status. The policy of the *Evening Citizen*, he noted, was to cover any advisory council reports when they were presented to the city council.

Race became an issue too when a black press council member asked if it was the newspaper's policy to display conspicuously crime news involving blacks. Such news, she said, invariably seemed to appear on page one.

The newspaper's policy, Brown replied, did not call for giving special display to crime news involving blacks. The broader policy of the newspaper was that all crime news normally appeared on page one. Later in the same meeting, Brown noted that the *Evening Citizen* had begun publishing a syndicated series about black history and spoke in a concerned way about the lack of knowledge of black history among white children and adults. The black aspect of American history has been largely ignored, he said, and black children frequently have had no one to admire.

Titled "The Last American" and featuring a sketch with brief text, the series drew high praise from the council members. One black council member, a teacher and administrator in the city's school system, said the historical series was extremely well done, combining high interest with an appropriate reading level. "We need more articles like this," said the educator. "Many of our problems are not of hatred, but of misunderstanding and ignorance."

Over the years, the *Evening Citizen* has treated local racial turmoil, including outbursts of violence, in a subdued manner. This often resulted in criticism from all sides. Even before 1954, the year of the Supreme Court's school desegregation ruling, the paper carried news of the black community. But it consisted largely of obituaries and a few social items. Until 1962, Negroes were specifically identified by race. Then, when racial trouble flared up in 1962, the paper began using photographs of blacks in news columns, to the displeasure of many white readers. As coverage of the black community grew, blacks began submitting news items. Black funeral directors once believed there was a charge for printing obituaries and made no effort to report them. The 1962 crisis brought business to a standstill, and some white businessmen, angered by coverage of racial issues, withheld advertising.

"The loss for us amounted to about $7000," recalled Brown. "There were pressures for us to stop reporting all racial trouble. Afterward, we were generally praised for our coverage. It was not sensationalized. I have a great deal of faith in the average reader. Sometimes the newspaper has not been performing what one would call a thoroughly professional job. The main reason is economics. If it were possible financially, it would certainly be feasible to hire another city reporter."

The hot summer of 1967 again brought racial trouble. And again the newspaper tried to report what was happening. Again, both whites and blacks were angry. But this time there were no economic pressures from the business community.

"We played it honestly, objectively, as fairly as we knew how," said Brown. "We didn't hide anything, but we did play it down.

There were no pictures, not even of the damage. They [blacks] wanted it blown up [emphasized]."

On one occasion, a photograph aroused the ire of council members, both black and white. Noting that the *Evening Citizen* had given excellent coverage to the city's recreation program, the council could not understand why a page-one photo showed only four of the seven key citizens involved in the program—all white. The three not shown were black, a member reported. The caption had noted in the last sentence: "Present at this meeting but not visible in the picture were other supervisors, including Johnnie Bond, Cleveland Forbes, and Bob Petrie." A white council member commented, "This is typical."

Brown responded that only two of the three not shown were blacks; the other was white. "The picture," he continued, "was taken in a room that was very small, and the individuals were asked who were the key persons so the picture could be taken." The key persons, it turned out, were those in the photograph.

What's (or Who's) News?

"What is news?" a council member asked. "I thought it was supposed to be something new, something not generally known. Is it necessary to repeat information in stories that has appeared in previous stories?"

She was referring to a report in the *Evening Citizen* which told of the replacement of an ousted public official. The man was black, was generally regarded as militant, and had been involved with the police in several Illinois communities. The beginning of the story, headlined *Named Area Coordinator of Migrant Council*, dealt with the replacement. The last paragraphs recounted charges brought against the ousted man in a recent case. The issue: Was it necessary to repeat charges against the Negro, even though an earlier story had cited them?

Yes, the last paragraph was relevant to the story, five council members voted.

No, it was not relevant to the story, countered the ballots of five other council members.

Brown said that reporters often end stories with facts from previous stories to provide background.

When trouble erupts in Cairo and the broadcast networks and

wire services become interested enough to send in newsmen, many residents, both black and white, cringe. Council members related eye-witness accounts of incidents that were "staged" by visiting newsmen.

"They wanted television pictures of a demonstration," said one member. "But there wasn't a demonstration so they staged one. What I'd like to know, is this kind of 'made' or 'managed' news quite common? Isn't there any kind of law against this?"

While council members castigated television—particularly CBS News—they frequently decried the *Evening Citizen's* failure even to cover some stories and incidents that members considered to merit stories.

"There may be a number of errors that appear in the news columns," said a member. "But the greatest error, in my estimation, is that of omission. Nothing could be printed in the newspaper that's half as bad as what's said on the street."

"It could be because of the racial situation," suggested a black councilwoman, recalling a recent incident in which a Cairo policeman had Maced a local Negro woman. "I first read about it in the East St. Louis newspaper. The story appeared here several days after the woman had been Maced—and only after the policeman accidentally Maced himself. And the purpose of the story then was to explain that Mace is not harmful after all, as the policeman could now testify. Why didn't the first story get in about the Negro woman getting Maced? People need to know about these problems."

Brown explained some of the limitations in gathering news, in addition to the pressure of deadlines and a limited staff. "Getting stories is not always easy. Often we have to be enterprising. Sometimes we're criticized for not having a particular story, but it may well be that we just cannot get the information for the story. Rumors must be sifted through in order to give us the information which we think gives us the true picture."

Later, he again addressed this issue: "We're covering a particularly difficult time in our history, maybe the most trying time in our history. The newspaper has not covered some things. It's difficult to get at something like that [quashing rumors]. Some things are better unsaid. Maybe some could say that we have compromised ourselves."

Brown indicated that his decisions were motivated by an effort to help bring some reason to a chaotic situation.

Council Reaction

At their seventh session, council members both bore down on their criticism of the *Evening Citizen* and candidly addressed themselves to this question: What effect had the press council had on the *Evening Citizen*?

"No difference," observed one.

"No effect at all," said another. "Like water off a duck's back."

"We have become more sympathetic to the problems of the newspaper," said another. "But I've noticed little, if any, difference in the paper over the past few months."

Within two months the mood of the members shifted. After disappointment at seeing so many of their suggestions brushed aside or glossed over, they began noticing some changes.

"There seems to be a lot more local news on that front page," commented one. (A persistent criticism had been that not enough local news appeared on page one.)

"There aren't as many corrections appearing in the newspaper," said another. "Maybe the newspaper has been more careful in its treatment of news."

"And the [local] editorials—they're the first thing I turn to now," added a third.

Why the sudden shift—in council members' attitudes as well as, apparently, in the paper?

Perhaps a meeting that took place on a July afternoon at Pere Marquette State Park provides part of the answer. Martin Brown and two council members had been invited to discuss their experience at the annual conclave of the International Conference of Weekly Newspaper Editors. Later, at the last regular session of the Cairo press council, Brown shared his thoughts about that meeting.

I began to realize during that meeting that more and more questions were being directed at me. The questions were about how the newspaper should react to criticism. If the reaction by the newspaper to council criticism is negative, will this jeopardize the whole idea? Will it fall apart? Well, it hasn't. One of the reasons we went back to local editorials was the impetus of the press council. The council has made us aware of some of the community problems and made us look at them in different ways.

ᐟAfter the last regularly scheduled council meeting, each member was asked, confidentially, to evaluate the experience. Most agreed that the council had yielded beneficial results, although several pointed to weaknesses.

"We have many problems," a black responded, "not the least of which is a lack of communication between the races. The council provided an excellent atmosphere for intelligent discussion of some of the local problems and complaints, with members of both races participating."

"Evidently," said another, "the management of the *Evening Citizen* has been stimulated sufficiently toward improving itself. There has always been available in their organization the inherent ability to produce superior editorials, and they are just beginning to mine their talented staff. . . . I believe that the Cairo Press Council presented a challenge which was necessary to start the ball rolling."

Nearly all agreed that the exchanges with Brown had helped bring about greater understanding of the problems involved in the production of a newspaper. This seemed to remove the sting from some of their original criticisms. In Brown's view, this resulted in a public relations function for the newspaper in that the council "helped many persons in Cairo to better understand the newspaper's problems of gathering and reporting the news daily."

But there were weaknesses too. Many agreed that a broader representation of the various segments of the community was necessary for the council to function more effectively. One council member felt discussion focused too heavily on the race issue, and several others indicated that discussion too frequently strayed from the purpose of the press council. "Sometimes I wondered what committee was meeting," confided one member.

Perhaps another weakness was the decision at the outset—for observational purposes—to limit publicity about the council's function and proceedings. As a result, members received little feedback from other citizens concerning the press council.

Newspaper Response

It is possible to document several changes that did occur in the newspaper. Unknown to Martin Brown, a content analysis was made of the *Evening Citizen*, beginning with issues published during the three months immediately before the first meeting and extending to one month beyond the last.[7] The analysis, which covered thirteen months divided into four periods, disclosed the number of local editorials appearing during each period: 1 of the total of 31 editorials, 0 of 33, 1 of 27, and 12 of 22. Clearly, the council had persuaded Brown that his paper should try to exert editorial leadership.

The other question to be answered by content analysis involved another frequent criticism: too little local news on page one. The proportion of the total front-page space devoted to local stories for each of the four periods was: 32.1 percent, 23 percent, 33.3 percent, and 37.9 percent. Although this change is less dramatic than for editorials, it also indicates that the editor heeded the complaints of the council. The analysis also indicated that the newspaper responded favorably to the council members' wishes for more education news, although there was a decline in the amount of coverage given to two other areas in which the council expressed an interest—news about government and civic organizations.

Did the editor feel that he had surrendered editorial authority? Not at all, Brown said. "As a publisher I would assure another publisher not to worry about the loss of control or any inroads as to management's decision which a press council might make. A press council is purely advisory."

Aftermath

On September 3, 1968, the Cairo press council met in a local restaurant and decided to organize on a permanent basis. But the group never met again. Racial tension mounted anew, and by the spring of 1969, in the midst of firebombing and gun battles on the streets, National Guard troops entered the beleaguered city to enforce calm. Since then, some 200 incidents of gunfire have occurred, many of them involving the police; and the predominantly black United Front instigated a boycott of white businesses which has run more than two years, one of the longest in the history of American race relations.[8]

The apparent spark for the latest outbreaks of violence was a revelation by a Catholic priest of the existence of an organization known as the White Hats, formally called the Committee of Ten Million. According to a document released by the city's Chamber of

Commerce "Truth Squad," the organization consisted of a group of "responsible citizens who have volunteered to serve as Deputies for either the sheriff or the Chief of Police. . . . They are men who have no other purpose than that of protecting their homes, businesses and families."[9] The priest, affiliated with the United Front, branded the organization a vigilante group that intimidated and terrorized black residents. (Although the White Hats were disbanded, a similar group called United Citizens for Community Action was founded.) The lieutenant governor of Illinois visited the city, and in a seven-page report called the communications breakdown between blacks and whites "almost unbelievable for a community of its size."[10]

That a press council made up of both blacks and whites even managed to survive a year in such a disturbed city was remarkable in itself. Obviously, some communication had occurred between the council members and newspaper management. But certainly a press council cannot be expected to undo a situation nurtured by hundreds of years of social turmoil. A question intrudes: Would a press council years ago have helped to alleviate the problems of today?

A year and a half after the council's last meeting, the *Evening Citizen* was sold to David C. Cain and Associates. After years of frustration, Martin Brown, with his family, moved from the city.

Notes

[1] Charles Dickens, *American Notes,* in *The Works of Charles Dickens,* Vol. 11 (New York: National Library Edition, no date), p. 223.

[2] John W. Allen, *Legends & Lore of Southern Illinois* (Carbondale, Ill.: Southern Illinois University Area Services Division, 1963), pp. 287-89.

[3] Robert E. Knittel, "An Evaluation of the Reliability of the Self-Study Method in Community Development," unpublished Ph.D. dissertation, Southern Illinois University, 1967, p. 41.

[4] Malcolm L. Comeaux, "Impact of Transportation Activities upon the Historical Development of Cairo, Illinois," unpublished A.M. thesis, Southern Illinois University, 1966, pp. 129-30.

[5] Albert Jene Shafter, "Old Town—New Town: A Study of the Factor Complexes Influencing the Development of Municipal Service Functions in Two Southern Illinois Cities," unpublished A.M. thesis, Southern Illinois University, 1949, p. 13.

[6] Basic Systems, Inc., *A Demographic Analysis of Poverty in the State*

of Illinois, prepared for the Illinois Office of Economic Opportunity, February 1965, p. 148.

[7]Howard R. Long and Kenneth Starck, "Pilot Demonstration on Developing Community Press Councils in Southern Illinois," report prepared for the Mellett Fund for a Free and Responsible Press, October 1969.

[8]"Cairo, Illinois: A Town in Troubled Waters," *Community Development Newsletter*, Southern Illinois University at Carbondale, May-June 1971.

[9]"The Cairo Story and How It Could Happen to You!", the Cairo Chamber of Commerce Truth Squad, Cairo, April 18, 1969 (mimeographed).

[10] *Southern Illinoisan*, April 22, 1969, p. 1.

CHAPTER SIX

Confrontation in St. Louis

by EARL REEVES

If the idea of democracy should ever be invalidated, it would be because it came about that more and more people knew less and less that was true about more and more that was important.

—Willard Wirtz

If the Cairo press council devoted much of its time to race problems, the Community Communications Council of St. Louis was even more sharply focused. Its mission was to establish a dialogue between St. Louis blacks and the news media.

The need was obvious. In St. Louis and elsewhere, blacks demand a stronger voice in decision making. The cry for "black power" is not new, but it is being sounded with a greater sense of urgency as blacks challenge the white world. Change is occurring. Doors are being forced open and the channels through which power can be developed and directed are being established. Many more blacks are winning elective positions on school boards and city councils, as well as in state legislatures and in Congress.

But one of the most important aspects of the development of power and influence is the ability to communicate effectively. If blacks are to become full and equal members of the urban community, they must be able to participate in discussing and analyzing community issues through the major news media.

The recent violence and rioting have forced awareness of how little is known or understood about the lives and problems of black Americans. Many serious questions have been raised:

—To what extent do the communications media provide adequate coverage of the social, cultural, and political news of the black community?

—To what extent does the search for the exciting and spectacular overemphasize incidents involving violence or threats of violence?

—Does inadequate news coverage block normal patterns of communication for blacks and stimulate rallies and even riots to call attention to their frustrations and aspirations?

The 1968 report of the National Advisory Commission on Civil Disorders (the Kerner Commission) concluded that the knottiest problem is the failure of the media to report adequately the problems of ghetto residents. The commission held that the news media:

> ... have not communicated to the majority of their audience—which is white—a sense of the degradation, misery, and hopelessness of living in the ghetto. They have not communicated to whites a feeling for the difficulties and frustrations of being a Negro in the United States. They have not shown understanding or appreciation of—and thus have not communicated—a sense of Negro culture, thought or history.
>
> Equally important, most newspaper articles and most television programming ignore the fact that an appreciable part of their audience is black. The world that television and newspapers offer to their black audience is almost totally white, in both appearance and attitude. As we have said, our evidence shows that the so-called "white press" is at best mistrusted and at worst held in contempt by many black Americans.[1]

The increasing intensity of black frustration and outrage are forcing many institutions to reevaluate their roles, and the communications media are no exception. Part of this reevaluation has occurred at conferences on the mass media and race relations around the country. Many have provoked at least some reassessment of the nature of news coverage of the black community. These conferences have provided an opportunity for blacks to challenge the standards of the white-dominated news media. The tenor of one such conference is suggested by the following excerpts from a newspaper account:

> American news media must share much of the blame for the nation's racial crisis, an author and magazine writer who specializes in race relations told representatives of Missouri and Kansas newspapers here [Kansas City] last night. . . .
>
> "What the press has got to do now," he said, "if it is to retain any believability at all, is to realize that the rules of the

game are changed. No longer is it morally correct, if it ever was, to sit back and reflect the ideas and ideals of a white middle class."

He said the traditionally respectable symbols of authority, such as police and public officials, are often "partisans in a battle that must be reported fairly and that sometimes they are going to be the enemy of a free society."

"When this happens, the press has got to point out their transgressions and speak for the conscience of a nation, because if the press doesn't, who will? Quite likely, people with clubs and guns and Molotov cocktails."[2]

As valuable as such conferences are—and they do serve to articulate many of the problems—it is necessary to find some stronger means of establishing and deepening communications. The Center of Community and Metropolitan Studies at the University of Missouri—St. Louis pursued this goal through a community press council.

Selection of Participants

The St. Louis metropolitan area is served by a wide variety of news media, including two nationally known newspapers (the *Globe-Democrat* and the *Post-Dispatch*), a number of black newspapers, radio and television outlets for the major networks, and three black-oriented radio stations. The press council, designed to include the top-level managers of the major news media in St. Louis and broadly representative group of black leaders, was to provide a forum for free discussion of points of conflict between the media and the black community.

As director of the press council, I selected the participants and presided at all of the meetings. Deciding which news media representatives should be included was not too difficult. I invited the managing editors of the newspapers and the general managers of radio and television stations.

Dr. Earl Reeves was Professor of Political Science at the Center of Community and Metropolitan Studies at the University of Missouri-St. Louis when he wrote this chapter. He is now Director of Urban Studies at the University of Tulsa.

The participation of managing editors and general managers was regarded as crucial because they are the key decision makers and not only can discuss the role of their institutions with authority, but also can implement new ideas or programs. Although the enthusiasm with which these men approached the project varied considerably, they were cooperative and interested. They included the managing editors of the two metropolitan dailies, the editor of a Negro weekly, the general managers of two of the three network television outlets and the news director of the third, and the general managers of three radio stations, including one black-oriented station.

Selection of the black participants was more complicated. In order to ensure that the black participants would be as representative as possible, I asked several black individuals and organizations to list those they felt should be included. The lists were combined (there was substantial overlap) and the number was pared to twelve, although two other blacks were added.

The black group included: the above-mentioned editor of a black newspaper; a prominent businessman who was also president of the St. Louis School Board; a member of the St. Louis Board of Aldermen who was also local president of the NAACP; the executive director of the Urban League; a psychiatrist; leaders of four community organizations (ACTION, Tandy Area Council, Mid-City Community Congress, and Carr-Central Neighborhood Association); a member of the Community Relations Service of the U.S. Department of Justice; and a student, the president of the Association of Black Collegians. The group contained both moderates and militants and was probably as representative as any small group could be, although no one from the Illinois side of the metropolitan area was included.

The plan called for a series of dinner meetings every three or four weeks throughout the summer, involving all participants and providing an opportunity to discuss important issues. But the program evolved differently.

Black Suspicion

The first meeting was a valuable introductory session in which a variety of issues were tentatively explored. The discussion began in an atmosphere of suspicion, with a sharply phrased question from one of the black members who wanted to know how much money was in the budget for the project and why the site was a downtown hotel rather than a black-owned restaurant where "Fannie May" could get the money. He was informed about the budget and was told that the group should help decide the location of future meetings.

One white participant commented that the black who asked the question did not seem to be enjoying the dinner, and suggested that he might be more comfortable eating where he could get soul food.

The black reacted bitterly: "I suppose you think that I'm afraid to eat with white people. Well, I'm not afraid to eat with white people, or those who are just about white."

The black businessman at whom this last barb seemed to be aimed demanded, "What do you mean by that?" "You ought to know, Uncle Tom," was the reply. "You are a living freak, a white mind in a black body."

At this point, the black newspaper editor intervened: "Name-calling doesn't help. Some of us have lived longer than others and have had some success. I'm not ashamed that I can support my family, but this doesn't mean I have lost touch." Then, turning to the newsmen, he charged: "As long as civil rights were in the South, news media coverage was good. But when it moved North and was no longer an academic question, things changed."

The general manager of one of the television stations defended the media: "TV has done a good job, but we want to hear your gripes. Ten years ago we started holding teen-age dances on TV. We were warned of problems that would occur if people saw Negroes and whites dancing together, but we went ahead with them and there have been no serious problems. Six years ago we did a program on Kinloch [an impoverished all-black municipality in St. Louis County] and we went to Washington to testify in favor of federal funds for Kinloch sewers. We also started a tutoring program and sought books for the library and school. We hired a Negro writer and producer for a show on employment problems, but we couldn't use him because he wasn't hard-hitting enough."

Disagreement among the black participants came up again when the head of the Urban League responded that he thought the news media were focusing too much attention on certain individuals and "interpreting demonstrations as the mood of the total community" when they really involved only a small number.

But the leader of ACTION (an organization well known for its vigorous though nonviolent protest) disagreed sharply: "If a person has cancer in a finger, it may be small, but it needs attention. Just because only one person protests doesn't mean it should be ignored."

He went on to charge that no one should expect the news media to tell the truth. "We must look at the composition of the news media. The news department must answer to someone. Stations must have ads, and ads come from the source that discriminates against black people. So the news is slanted. Stations might risk boycotting if they told the truth. Newsmen must be willing to be fired or suddenly demoted if they tell the truth."

He also charged news reports of crime and police action were one-sided and distorted. "Only the policeman's side is told. No attempt is made to interview the witnesses to get the other side."

The general manager of one of the TV stations asserted that, though the news media did receive pressure from advertisers, the "pressure is not on content but on circulation. New York [network headquarters] doesn't care what we show but how many are watching."

The black businessman challenged him, asking if he did not slant the news to get an audience. The black alderman added that he liked the Kerner Commission's emphasis on white racism: "This was a dramatic, honest statement. As long as TV is run by racists," he said, "the white establishment doesn't have to worrry, nor does it have to tell you what to say. The establishment knows you will reflect its views. These new racists don't believe in lynching or nonvoting or legal discrimination, but they have other hangups."

Why No Black Reporters?

The black alderman pointed out that there are no black faces in the editorial rooms of the *Post* or the *Globe*. "You newsmen are racists. I don't mean that you hate Negroes, but you live in a white world. It's not the fault of the press—it's the fault of the entire country. But the press could do something about it."

Some of the news media representatives protested that they were trying to recruit black staff members. "We ran ads for newsmen, but there was only one black out of 136 applicants, and he wasn't qualified," a news director said.

The director of the Urban League asked whether the newsman

was willing to take a Negro with less education and train him. And the black editor pointed out that the trade publications in which ads are placed don't reach the Negroes. Then he asked, "How does a man get the experience he needs to work for you?"

The news director replied that small towns are the chief recruiting grounds. "That's where you get experience, and you work your way up to a station in a major metropolitan area."

The black psychiatrist protested that "Negroes can't get a job in a small town to get experience." And the black editor noted bitterly: "Even when experienced, qualified blacks are available, you won't use them. When I was with the U.S. Information Agency, they were having trouble developing a documentary on Negroes. I tried to get them to use a Negro advisor. I gave them names, like Lerone Bennett [senior editor of *Ebony* magazine and author of *Before the Mayflower*], but they wouldn't do it. That is why Negroes are frustrated. We all suffer the same damn thing. We are all in the same pot. This is what racism means."

The black school board president said that "the newspapers only contact me when they have a question about race; they never ask me about finance, curriculum, or other subjects. I guess they don't think a Negro knows anything about them."

"In an institution," the managing editor of one of the newspapers admitted, "things don't always go according to your wishes. White racism *is* the problem. We are trying to hire Negro reporters, but the competition from TV and government is terrific. We have a scholarship at the University of Missouri—Columbia which is given to Negroes. We hope to hire them, but so far no payoff. We have even tried hiring some without a good knowledge of English, but it didn't work out."

Black Power and Black Separatism

At the second meeting participants attempted to define such controversial terms as "black power," "black nationalism," and "law and order." They began by discussing whether the word "black" should replace the word "Negro."

The black businessman said that the word "black" now "really seems to be acceptable as a definition of who we are—but the news media have made it a dirty word." Then, turning to the black psychiatrist, whose skin color was a light brown, he said: "A few years ago you would probably have been offended to be called black, but today we can feel a sense of unity as black men." The psychiatrist agreed that he could now acknowledge his "blackness."

But the black editor disagreed. "There is still much resentment to 'black,' " he said. "Some older Negroes still resent the term."

The black businessman, however, insisted that "black" was increasingly acceptable, and that, in fact, the concept of "the dignity of being black" was the key to the development of an all black-owned supermarket established in St. Louis. The black woman in the group put the issue this way: "When whites resent the term 'black power' the problem is the word 'power,' and not the word 'black.' Whites fear the term for fear of losing their power."

A white newsman asked what "black nationalism" and "black power" meant. Others expressed confusion over the apparent emphasis on separatism after so many years with integration as the goal. One black responded that "black power" was simply the desire for control, because a person could not be free if he had no control over what happened to him.

Another contended the black had to gain freedom for himself. "White Americans are not free," he argued, "so they cannot give freedom. Black nationalism is a philosophy that grants a kind of freedom and unity. Freedom comes only through nationalism—not physical, but psychological separation. I can look at my woman and know that she is good, and I don't have to want your woman. Black nationalism means self-respect."

If "black power" disturbed the white participants, the term "law and order" disturbed the blacks. When one of the white newspapermen asked about law and order, the community organization leader from the Mid-City Community Congress responded sharply, asking why justice could not be the focus. "Hitler had law and peace," he argued. "We spend too much on arms and not enough on food and welfare. Racists are heading congressional committees. A man like [Senator] Eastland is on welfare [receiving soil-bank payments], while others starve."

The black businessman pointed out bitterly that "the white man has been breaking laws for 300 years. Now, when the Negro begins to move, you suddenly cry for law and order."

Then the Mid-City leader pulled a match from his pocket, lit it, and held it high. "You see how fascinated you are by fire. I can call a meeting of black businessmen in my office to talk about some constructive project and you won't pay any attention at all. But if I announce that we are going to burn down Franklin Avenue, then every newspaper and television station in town will have their reporters there. You force us to make these statements in order to get your attention."

Am I a Racist?

The attempt to define racism also led to an entangled discussion. While the blacks were speaking of a white racist *system*, the whites interpreted references to racism as a personal attack. This dialogue illustrated the problem:

> *White News Director:* Am I personally guilty just for being white?
> *Mid-City Community Leader:* We have a racist system. The best white man is still a racist. The system is set up so that only a few Negroes make it. It is a hope system. A few make it, so there is hope. But black people are further behind than they were ten years ago.
> *White News Director:* Why am I guilty?
> *Black Psychiatrist:* There was a famous rape case a few years ago in which the police arrested 100 blacks to find five Negro rapists. There actually hadn't even been a rape.
> *Black Editor:* I was working for the *Argus* [a black newspaper]. We called for swift justice. Negroes were called cannibals by the white press. The ghetto was said to be just like the Congo. Then it was found that the woman was lying. She was sick and the white community turned on her. After the news media found out she had lied, they referred to five *men*, not five Negroes. The problem is that you whites are so much a part of the system that you feel no guilt. Even many black people are part of the system.

But the white news director was still thinking of racism in terms of Jim Crow laws, which he had consistently opposed. "What if you have spent most of your professional life fighting the system and then you are called a racist?", he demanded.

The response from the black psychiatrist did not help: "The most dangerous person of all is the liberal who gets mad; even a fascist is better."

The black businessman again asked, "Why have the news media treated black power like thay have when it has provided unity for the Negro?"

One white newspaper editor insisted, however, that "the press didn't make it derogatory. It was the action that accompanied it. Stokely Carmichael caused the trouble. Every time he used the term it was followed by violence."

The black psychiatrist reacted sharply. "That statement is a *non sequitur*. It reminds me of one of my paranoid patients who always feels he is being followed. There is nothing wrong with black power; it makes me feel good."

The discussion again turned to racism and what the news media had done to combat it. This dialogue, too, suggests how difficult it was for blacks and whites to communicate.

Black Student: The forefathers started a fine country, but they also brought black people here and pushed them down. They made black evil. But now we're getting over that hump.

White TV Manager: It is not enough to say it is our fault because our fathers did it. What is important is our present intention.

Black Student: But what have you done? We've been here 350 years, but we are strangers. White students don't know anything about us.

White TV Manager: The media have mushroomed. When I grew up I didn't know what happened in the South. Today we know everything instantly. The impact of the news media today is creating a generation of more broad-minded people. I just can't believe that we aren't doing something.

Carr-Central Community Leader: The problem is not just in the South. The whole society is racist. The North is worse. In the South, at least, Negroes had jobs, even though at the bottom. In the North, black men are jobless, powerless.

Black Businessman: We've had 300 years of degrading the black male, destroying the black family.

Second White TV Manager: What are the rights you want?"

Mid-City Community Leader: If the news media were really doing their thing, they could change the image [of the black man]. You are making motions, but you aren't putting your heart into it.

White Radio Manager: I think we are. There are Negro models in commercials on TV and radio now.

Black Businessman: Negroes are in commercials for the economic benefit they bring you. Why can't Sammy Davis, Jr. lead a TV program? He lasted less than a year, with all of his ability. If Madison Avenue wanted to, they could make it work.

Second White TV Manager: I get the feeling that whatever we do is wrong.

Black Businessman: No, nothing personal. We know that if there weren't some good white people there would be no hope.

A Distorted Image

The black participants charged that there is blatant discrimination and distortion in news about blacks, citing the coverage of Adam Clayton Powell as an example. They felt his problems were a result of the news media's "determination to get him." As the black psychiatrist put it, "For all his faults, the news media could have told the truth about Adam. He was no worse than a lot of the white congressmen. Why did the media pick on him? I don't think you are really honest. You just toy with the Negro community."

The blacks also charged that the media tend to overemphasize black crime. One white editor replied that the papers simply covered the news, and that the ghetto, after all, is where most crimes occur. But, blacks pointed out, retail stores have their highest loss from pilferage in the suburbs—a fact that is never reported.

The system, the blacks insisted, makes the poor look bad. If they have a larger number of illegitimate births, for example, it is quite simply because they can't afford abortions. The net result of the system was a double standard on crime reporting which created a negative image of the black man. For example, the blacks pointed out, when, the day before, the transmitter of a black-oriented St. Louis radio station was bombed, the news media immediately assumed it was done by militants who had been demanding time to present their ideas on this station. In effect, the media proclaimed the blacks guilty.

The *Post-Dispatch*

Since attendance at the second meeting had been much lower than at the first, it was suggested that the media representatives might be more comfortable if the blacks met with members of only a single newspaper or radio or television station. The third meeting therefore took place in the boardroom of the St. Louis *Post-Dispatch* and involved black participants and the paper's top news executives, including the executive editor, managing editor, the editorial page editor, the city editor, and the women's editor. This encouraged specific discussion of the role of a newspaper and provided an atmosphere in which the editors could talk more freely.

The black alderman chided the editors for having "tired blood," charging they were weary of the civil rights struggle and would like to see it go away. "You go along with civil rights, but you seem to have lost your enthusiasm. Why don't you report what is really going on? Why don't you have any top-flight Negro columnists?"

Defending the paper, the executive editor insisted: "There is no partnership between our paper and the black community. We are in partnership with human rights. We have done it long before the activist. We report everything we consider significant and meaningful to the community."

But what was meant by "significant"? "There is nothing significant in today's paper about Negroes," the black alderman said.

"Yes, there is," the executive editor responded. "There is an article on page one about a riot in Peoria. Also, the general news is of concern to the Negro community."

The discussion continued thus:

Carr-Central Community Leader: But there is a real fight going on in our neighborhood about housing. We are trying to get approval for some land to build housing which would take 260 families out of the ghetto. But you ignored the story even though we sent in a press release.

ACTION Community Leader: Perhaps we don't understand your definition of news. What is the guideline?

Executive Editor: News is what is important, significant to the people who read.

ACTION Leader: But that is by white standards, not black.

Tandy Area Community Leader: Why don't you have any articles on public officials who own slum property?

Executive Editor: We are currently looking into this matter.

Black Alderman: You used to crusade for changes which were needed. There is so much that is wrong going on in St. Louis. Why aren't there any more crusades? We know you're worried about Vietnam, but what about St. Louis?

The women's editor said she was "trying to get away from stories on Negroes as Negroes. We have a feature coming up on African clothes." And she indicated that people with stories should call her.

"But if you had a black person on your staff, you wouldn't have to wait for a call," one black responded—and the debate went on:

Executive Editor: We want a black person on the staff. Ten years ago we hired a Negro reporter and later we had another one, but they were hired away. We *want* Negro reporters and editors.

ACTION Community Leader: Your basic mistake is that you think in terms of hiring *one*. You need to hire in volume.

Executive Editor: We would be glad to hire in volume.

Black Alderman: You may have to go out and buy someone if you really want a top-flight person. Look at *Ebony*, the federal government, etc., and find someone. Don't just limit yourself to cub reporters.

Executive Editor: We are under some economic limitations.

Black Businessman: But you are a prestige newspaper. You ought to be able to hire a black assistant city editor.

Executive Editor: It's not that easy. It is traditional with this newspaper for executives to come up through the ranks.

Black Businessman: But Negroes haven't even been able to get into the ranks. Do we have to wait twenty-five years for some cub reporter to rise to a policy-making position?

ACTION Community Leader: You must see the importance of the newspaper on public opinion. White people think they know Negroes, but they don't.

Editorial Page Editor: We want to do better.

Mid-City Community Leader: Have you gone to other cities on a talent hunt for Negroes?

Executive Editor: We have talked to people from *Jet* and *Ebony*. We have contacted the journalism schools for Negro talent. Besides, our reputation is good enough that a lot of people come to us. We don't ask about their color.

Managing Editor: We also have contacted the national Urban League.

Mid-City Community Leader: You need someone who understands the life style of the black community. You could use a man like the black editor in this group.

ACTION Community Leader: Reporters are what is important right now. I am convinced that there is talent right here in St. Louis.

Carr-Central Community Leader: But we also need black editors so the black reporters' material isn't junked.

Another black leader turned the discussion to a different tack: "If we are going to solve the old problems we need something new. Would you be willing to run a series of articles on what people think who live in the ghetto?"

The executive editor said he would welcome articles written by ghetto people. In fact, he said, prospective contributors could come in and tell their stories to a reporter, or tape them and a reporter could write them up for them.

But, said the blacks, would the reporter tell it straight or distort the black man's ideas? Could a black person review the article before it was printed?

An editor replied that reporters never allowed subjects to approve articles before publication. Nevertheless, it was finally agreed that a ghetto resident should approve an article appearing under his by-line before it was printed.

Asked who should receive the articles, the executive editor said he should. At that, the Carr-Central leader asked, "How do we know that someone at the top won't stop the article?"

The executive editor replied that any article he accepted would be published.

The black participants seemed to feel that this agreement opened the door to progress. As one acknowledged, "You are trying to be honest, and we are just trying to show you another point of view. Editors need roots in a community."

The managing editor commented that the session had been very helpful. "I have ultimate responsibility for what goes into the news columns," he said. "But I didn't realize until now that you thought we were falling off the wagon."

The meeting concluded with the blacks expressing their apprecia- tion but again emphasizing the need for articles "which not only discuss problems but also consider our ideas for solutions."

Television and the Question of Context

After a few abortive attempts, another press council meeting was arranged with the staff of KSD-TV (the NBC outlet in St. Louis), including the station's program director, news director, assistant news director, sales manager, and three newsmen.

The two-and-a-half-hour discussion began with the problem of how ghetto people could make the station aware of news which they felt was important. The black psychiatrist asked where the station got its leads for news stories, to which the news director replied that his staff used the police radio, press releases, and telephone calls.

The Tandy Area community leader then asked whether there was collusion among television stations to determine what was con- sidered news. He noted that his group had made a survey and issued a report on discriminatory food prices in the ghetto, but the news media had ignored it and had reported the contrary conclusions of a survey made by the Better Business Bureau. Asked if his group had contacted the news media or protested, the Tandy Area leader said that they had presented their case at a public meeting at which the Better Business Bureau's survey was discussed, but they had been ignored. One of the TV newsmen admitted that he had heard the charges and talked to experts, but, though skeptical, he had still reported the Bureau survey. This, the black psychiatrist pointed out, was a good example of the problem—which was one of credibility. "How," he asked, "do you decide who is trustworthy? Do you go to established institutions or just go free-swinging?"

Only a few weeks earlier, at Christmas, one black said, he and a group which included a white nun had picketed downtown stores as a "black Christmas" protest, seeking to illustrate the exploitation of blacks by white merchants at Christmas time. Several people, including the leader, were arrested, but only the white nun was interviewed by the press.

A reporter pointed out that the arrest of a nun was certainly news.

"Of course it is," the black replied. "That's why she was with us. But you didn't have to ignore the rest of us, and you didn't have to ignore our message. Why do you think we get arrested? Do you think it's fun? We're trying to tell you something, and all you do is focus on the arrest and ignore the story."

Though the program director argued that there was no plan to ignore, the reporters acknowledged there was a problem. "I'm learning," one admitted. "I realize there is much I don't understand. We do the best we can."

"We really don't know who the leaders are," a second reporter confessed. "We don't know who to go to. We go to the people we know."

The black community relations man responded that this empha-sized the need for a mechanism whereby "you can really get some soundings."

The ACTION leader asked why he had never been interviewed. A reporter said that he had wanted to interview him, but had been overruled by his superiors. The program director took exception, although he admitted that the reporter might have been restricted on a particular story.

One reporter suggested that militants were not interviewed because the station did not want to report news that would be detrimental to blacks. Someone asked, "What is a militant?"

Someone like the ACTION leader, the reporter responded. "Someone who is active and believes in black nationalism."

The Tandy Area leader asked if being a "militant" was wrong.

A second reporter replied: "If it is separatist, it is."

The black student charged that the reporters used the word "militant" to discredit blacks. "I don't consider myself a 'black' militant," he said. "You don't call George Washington a 'white' militant. The word 'militant' conjures up evil thoughts—Stokely [Car-michael] is called a militant, and so nothing he does is right."

A reporter then asked if Stokely Carmichael should be on TV, stating that Carmichael had triggered the April 1968 Washington, D.C. riot. Two or three blacks objected almost in chorus that the Washington riot couldn't be blamed on Carmichael, that he was just sounding a warning.

One black asked what standards the media used to determine which black groups were making news. A reporter responded that the press couldn't cover every demonstration. The ACTION leader countered that though he was aware of this, he also knew that many paper organizations made news while many substantial groups were ignored. "We know you can't cover everything," he said, "but how do you order your priorities?"

The reporter answered that the crucial factor was how many people a group represented. Another pointed out that the NAACP criticized the press for interviewing militants who represented only a few people. The first reporter agreed "there is a real danger that we will build up the wrong people."

A black stated that newsmen didn't seem to worry about building up the wrong person when they dealt with whites.

The reporter then made a startling admission: "Many things are not covered because *we think* they are not good for the black community"—unintentionally illustrating the charge that black news *was*, in fact, being subjectively interpreted through white eyes.

Someone asked why the blacks were willing to support "militants" who were offending whites just when real progress was being made in race relations. The black community relations worker replied, "There are a lot of angry people, and to them any cat that makes white people uncomfortable is a hero. There are people who are so angry that they are not satisfied with negotiations. They want to assert their manhood."

The program director agreed that whites must wake up and face the facts, assuring the group, "We're trying. You must know this."

The black community relations man acknowledged this, but cautioned: "One of the problems of this kind of session is that the black cat is so frustrated that he will seem hostile to you when he really isn't."

The ACTION leader added, "We're trying to be honest and not just be nice. We aren't talking out of animosity."

The next question raised was how news coverage could be

improved. The TV station sales manager commented that "the most important thing is context. We do focus on black news, but we need the context."

This again led to discussion of the need for black journalists. As one of the blacks stressed, "You've got to have a guy who is in the community every day who knows what is going on in the ghetto."

The black student agreed. Even though he was leader of a black organization, he pointed out, he had to work to keep up: "If I don't keep right up to date, I lose out."

The program director named a black girl he had tried to hire and asked if she was the type of person that ought to be offered a job. "She would be excellent," the black student acknowledged. "She is in the movement enough to satisfy everybody."

But the ACTION leader objected. "The best person for such a job is a man. Too often the door opens to black females. To black people this is an insult. We need males to identify with."

The program director admitted he hadn't even thought of this. Another black stated that the girl was the caliber of person needed, but a man would be better. The black student suggested that, to meet qualified people, the broadcaster should talk to black college students. The ACTION leader summed up by saying that the station could impress the black community by hiring and developing a local person. "There must be a Jackie Robinson in St. Louis somewhere."

The meeting ended there, but in the informal discussion that followed, the newsmen gained some more insight into black frustrations and added names to their list of news sources. The black participants learned more about the operations of a television news department and met the news director and others who would welcome ideas and news items.

Wrap-up

About two weeks after this session, I sent a preliminary report on the project to all participants. One week later, at the final dinner meeting, the participants gave their reactions.

The black student and the managing editor of the St. Louis *Post-Dispatch* presented prepared statements. These statements are quoted here in their entirety because they summarize the two basic opposing views of the role of the news media. The student spoke first:

The most serious problems of the news media are interpretation and intent. The only way to conquer the interpretation gap is to hire black minds. The news media must make a conscious effort to de-brainwash and reeducate the American people. This reeducation will only be accomplished by intensive and sustained coverage of every phase of the human aspects of black Americans. The *Report of the National Advisory Commission on Civil Disorders* advises the media to immediately hire black reporters and staff. But most important, it suggests that the media begin recruiting. The media must take the initiative and find promising high school students. These students should be offered scholarships in journalism. The media should also look in our colleges and universities.

St. Louis is about 40 percent black. The media should attempt to give the black community come sort of commensurate coverage. The media will have to do some things which go against traditions. But traditions have always been against black men. In order to make things change, we must change things. We must begin to do that which has not been done previously. The media will know when they have succeeded in becoming relevant when black people see in the papers and programs the evidence of their humanness.

From the research I have done, I feel that the media must reexamine the myth of their supposed objectivity. The media are predispositioned and all of their expertise cannot rule out their conscious and subconscious racism. The media must resolve to intentionally give the black community a positive human image.

Finally, I feel that as far as the black side of this project was concerned, black youth was underrepresented. The black youth of today is very much in with the whole black movement. Sooner than most people realize, the new thinking youth in the black community will be the man who must be bargained with.

The managing editor of the *Post-Dispatch* then spoke:

Trying to speak as a dispassonate and impartial observer, it seems to me that the Mellett Fund sessions proved again what everybody working in this area has found out—namely, the extreme difficulty, if not impossibility, of overcoming rapidly centuries of neglect, at best, and discrimination at worst. Instant changes in basic newspaper attitudes and systems is no more possible than is instant change in many other areas.

In one sense, what was at issue in the discussion is that well-kicked-around problem of compensatory treatment of blacks—which, of course, covers a much wider spectrum of American life than merely communications media.

We are just as unwilling to handle news differently for Negroes as we are for Jews, Catholics, Swedes, or any other distinct group in American society. Our entire orientation, our education, our ideals, our habits of thought have all been directed toward judging news and people on their own merits and on the significance of the event for the total community. At least some of the black participants, however, if I understood them correctly, seem to feel that we should hire large numbers of undereducated blacks, place blacks in responsible positions immediately, and do similar things we would never conside doing for any other group. Everything within me cries out to resist letting the *Post-Dispatch* get involved in such procedures.

Equally, however, everything within me cries out that the *Post-Dispatch* has the responsibility to lead in trying to promote opportunities for black advancement. This includes coverage of significant black news, reporting of achievements of distinguished blacks, and doing everything we can do to promote black employment in responsible positions on the *Post-Dispatch* staff.

I don't think any of us on the white side of the fence is willing to take a relatively inexperienced black man and make him an editor overnight. What we are willing to do is to fill vacancies with qualified black applicants when the opportunity arises. We can and have created a few special opportunities for blacks. I hope we will find ways to do more of this. We cannot, however, lower our standards and accept slovenly reporting or poor writing simply because the author is black. To do so would be a disservice to all our readers, black and white.

Unquestionably the discussions reflected an understandable difference of opinion about the urgency of instant elimination of racial problems. Although I think, perhaps mistakenly, that I am quite sympathetic to the black side of this controversy, I am unwilling to allow a general circulation newspaper like the

Post-Dispatch to become principally a civil rights organ, any more than I will let it become principally a publication for business, labor, sports, religion, or any other kind of special-interest news. Somebody who wants to read only news about civil rights will have to read it in publications devoted to this subject, as a businessman has to read the *Wall Street Journal* and a sportsman *Sports Illustrated*. We are concerned with attempting to report all the events of the day which are important or interesting to nearly all St. Louisans, not just some of them.

The Mellett Fund sessions have been most helpful to me in meeting some of the leaders of the black community. I don't think they have given me any new insights into black problems and black attitudes, although they may have reinforced some notions I had had previously. I think the most important results has been to open channels of communication which we have always believed were there but the blacks apparently did not.

Notes

[1] *Report of the National Advisory Commission on Civil Disorders* (New York: Bantam Books, 1968), p. 383.
[2] St. Louis *Post-Dispatch*, May 13, 1968.

CHAPTER SEVEN

Communication in St. Louis

by EARL REEVES

If the end doesn't justify the means, what does?

—Joseph Fletcher

The confrontation-discussion sessions in St. Louis raised far more questions than they answered. The separate meetings with the staff of a single newspaper or station seemed to pose the questions more sharply than did the large meetings. Perhaps this was because separate meetings permitted more focus; perhaps because when an executive was flanked by his key associates, it was possible to marshal more detailed information. Separate meetings also made media representatives less fearful of looking bad (or, worse, looking foolish) in the presence of their competitors. The last dinner meeting, with all of the media represented, almost came apart at the seams when representatives of two TV stations began arguing over which was more broad-minded and black-oriented.

The Frightening Gulf

Perhaps the most important result of the meetings was that they revealed a frighteningly wide gulf between the blacks and the newsmen —so wide that sometimes the two seemed to be speaking different languages. The concepts of "black power" and "black nationalism" had strikingly different connotations for the two groups. Although blacks did not always agree on the meaning of the terms, they felt "black" was the most acceptable definition of "who we are" and that "black power" basically represented a desire by blacks for "a piece of the action," for an opportunity to decide for themselves what was good for them. Combined with black nationalism, "black power" connoted a sense of black pride and unity—a sense that, however great their individual differences, black people share the experience of being shut out, of being subjected to a variety of indignities, of being branded as strangers in their own country because of the color of their skin. As the black editor said, "This is why Negroes are frustrated. We all suffer the same damn thing. We are all in the same pot. This is what racism means."

Black nationalism, it became clear, includes the idea of separatism; it was simply recognizing, blacks pointed out, the separatism which whites have decreed. Nonetheless, the concept of nationalism expressed in these discussions stressed psychological rather than physical separation. Black nationalism was defined in terms of self-respect and a sense of group solidarity.

To some of the white participants, however, these concepts implied violence, riots, and perhaps revolution. Asked why news media responded so negatively to "black power," which had unified Negroes, one of the editors replied, "The press didn't make it derogatory. It was the action that accompanied it. Every time Stokely Carmichael and Rap Brown used the term, it was followed by violence."

Often the rhetoric used in these discussions strengthened this interpretation. The blacks sometimes expressed their frustration in revolutionary terms that shocked the white listeners because they seemed to call for the overthrow of the system, and their language was sometimes couched in terms of fire and violence.

"White racism" proved to be so highly emotion-laden that it threatened to derail the discussion. When a black said that he agreed with the Kerner Commission's emphasis on white racism, he had to explain that white racism did not mean lynching, prevention of voting, or legal discrimination, but the absence of blacks from positions of significance. Time and again the blacks tried to indicate they were attacking the "system," not individuals. They emphasized that they were not charging the white participants with personal guilt but were trying to show that whites lived, worked, and thought in an essentially white world, without any real awareness of what it offered to blacks.

But "racist" seemed to the newsmen to be a term of personal attack and an implication of guilt that they were not willing to accept. They often expressed either a strained tolerance or open hostility at what they regarded as efforts to browbeat them into wearing a hair shirt of repentance for the sins of society. All this becomes more understandable in the light of political scientist Ralph W. Conant's views on "rhetoric and reality." Black rhetoric, he writes, tends to be most extreme when there is "no confidence in the group to which it is addressed, but as the level of confidence increases, the rhetoric becomes more realistic." Conant also warns that whites should not simply reject black symbolic rhetoric as absurd:

> White influentials who find themselves confronted with "black power" demands ordinarily reject them as unrealistic. What they mean by unrealistic is that the blacks who present them have no bargaining power. The demands themselves are, in the main, forms of control and influence which whites are quite used to having and exercising. What appears to be a demand for separatism is really a demand for local self-government, which is a cherished tradition in white America.[1]

The gulf between the blacks and journalists was revealed too in their sharp disagreement on the value of the present efforts of the news media. The newsmen believed they were already making significant efforts to report on and relate to the black community. But the black participants felt little had been done that indicated any real understanding. While agreeing that some limited progress had been made—the press had finally started capitalizing the word Negro and had eliminated the more flamboyant anti-Negro reporting—the blacks felt this was small comfort in view of the deeply entrenched racism of society.

Systematic Racism

The blacks asserted that much of the life in the black community was still ignored—that to judge by the society pages, for instance, blacks never married, bore children, or died, and that many other stories blacks felt important were never reported. Although this exclusion may be the result of ignorance—to many whites, blacks often seem not to exist—it has also partly been deliberate policy, especially in the media's failure to cover stories they did not consider "beneficial" to the black community.

This happened, for example, in conjunction with the Veiled Prophet Ball, an annual event which is the high point of St. Louis' social season but which to many blacks has symbolized their exclusion from American society. In response, a St. Louis civil rights group, led by a press council participant, organized a separate Black Veiled Prophet Ball, and issued press releases explaining the reason for it. The media did not cover the ball, however, and at the first council meeting, the newsmen were asked what it would take to get them to do so. Their reply was: "Get a good turnout of Negro leadership to prove that it was significant."

This provoked some bitter remarks about whites always having to find "responsible" Negro leaders. One black pointed out that the newspapers used to cover the Chauffeurs' Ball, which showed "Negroes in their place," without requiring the approval of "leaders." He added that the Black Veiled Prophet Ball certainly had broader black community support than had the Chauffeurs' Ball.

That journalists ignore news they feel isn't "beneficial" for blacks was a recurrent theme. It was cited by the black participants as illustrating systematic racism because it showed whites in positions of power deciding what was good for blacks. Moreover, they maintained, even when such news is covered, the stories may be subtly patronizing or insulting—as in a recent account of a black upper-middle-class debutante ball, the tone of which implied amazement that black debutantes could understand the social graces. Significantly, the managing editor of the paper involved acknowledged that the article was indeed patronizing and should never have been printed. He said he had ordered that no other article written in such a manner was to be published. (A few weeks later the paper printed a well-written report on a black debutante ball—although, as a black participant ruefully observed, it appeared in the news section instead of the society pages.)

The blacks also felt that because the news media are so oriented to the spectacular and the sensational, the only way blacks could gain attention was to stage demonstrations or threaten violence. In fact, they contended, many so-called radical and irresponsible statements and actions of black action groups were intended specifically to attract attention, but the result—especially with TV coverage and its rigid time constraints—was that the incident alone made news and the real message never got through. This, they said, increased tension, with the reporters viewing activists as publicity seekers and the blacks viewing reporters as part of a conspiracy of silence deliberately ignoring their grievances and suppressing their attempts to communicate.

One black contended that the media could not be expected to tell the truth because they were controlled by their advertisers. A newspaper editor replied that although advertisers sometimes attempted to exert control over news by withdrawing their ads, his paper printed the truth in spite of this. The general manager of a TV station added that the pressure he received from advertisers was not about news content but about how many viewers were watching.

Do the media slant the news in order to get the audience? The blacks contended that the St. Louis news media had done a fine job of reporting in the early '60s, when civil rights activity was limited to the South, but that when Martin Luther King went north and when racial unrest came to St. Louis, the coverage was less enthusiastic—the media, as one person put it, suddenly developed "tired blood."

The Quest for Context

In the entire discussion of news coverage, probably the most significant point made was this: Journalists decide what is news and how it should be covered on the basis of their own experience and background—and most newsmen lack the background and experience to really understand the black community.

Some white reporters acknowledged that a major problem in covering the black community was the difficulty in knowing the context. One newsman pointed out, however, that adding black faces to news staffs would not automatically guarantee better coverage, and the council agreed that any reporter, regardless of color, trying to cover the black community adequately had to spend time becoming acquainted with a variety of ghetto people (not just the formal leaders) and gaining insight into their problems.

Both blacks and journalists expressed frustration that the media had not developed reliable infomation sources in the black community. Too often, they agreed, reporters either contacted one of the handful of "safe" Negro leaders or followed a wandering firebrand and reported his more inflammatory statements. The result was a distorted picture which either ignored basic problems or depicted all blacks as running through the streets with gasoline cans screaming, "Burn, baby, burn!" A white newsman, participants felt, could develop the contacts for effective reporting if he was really permitted time to develop a relationship of trust with many news sources, although a black reporter obviously had an advantage in establishing such relationships.

It was pointed out that although most news executives recognize they must provide opportunities for black staff members, they insist they can't find qualified applicants to be reporters. And since editors normally begin as reporters, it is difficult for a black to reach an executive position in journalism. And with no black editors—or editors sensitive to the black community—even effective reporters, black or white, may find their stories on blacks weakened or filtered out in the editing process.

In essence, the blacks argued, the deck was stacked. A "color blind" hiring policy claiming to base employment strictly on merit would still screen out most blacks for lack of experience. The solution, the blacks insisted, was that the media should hire inexperienced but able black applicants and give them an opportunity to learn on the job.

The "Objectivity Fetish"

Perhaps the root of the problem of black news coverage was the journalists' insistence that their goal was objective treatment of the news of all groups, white or black. They reacted to many of the complaints and suggestions as special pleading and on several occasions voiced their fear of becoming "propaganda organs" for the black community.

U.C.L.A. journalism professor Jack Lyle, however, has called such thinking the "objectivity fetish":

> News editors and schools of journalism preparing reporters to work for these editors have stressed that reporters should tell the facts—"who, what, when, where, and how." "Why" cowers at the end of the list, for the reporter is not to indulge himself in interpretation—that is the domain of the editorial and column writer. Such objectivity is a myth; every witness, even the trained reporter, sees an event from particular points of view shaped by time, geographic location, and psychological filters of past experience. . . .
>
> Today many news executives have realized the paradox that the objective news report may be a more biased account of an event than an interpretive one. Emphasis is increasingly being placed on the training of specialized writers who can bring to a news report a background of not only expertise but also conti-

nuity, enabling them to report the event in a historical context. But traditions die slowly, and such specialization is expensive; meanwhile, the pressures of news volume grow. The result is that news continues to be action oriented, with little emphasis on explanation, little treatment of potential problems.[2]

As every press council meeting made clear, it is the sense of being ground down by the almost immutable pressures of tradition and inertia that frustrates and enrages black Americans. This is what they mean when they condemn the "racist system." They are not attacking the moral principles or the personal integrity of newsmen, nor are they even suggesting a sinister plot. They are emphasizing that traditional patterns exclude the black man, and therefore a solution to the racial crisis requires new directions by those in positions of influence.

The blacks consider the media crucial because of their strong influence in developing the frame of reference within which decisions are made. If black Americans are to have a chance to participate fully in American society, the news media must develop a greater awareness of the existence of blacks and their role in American life. Press councils like the one in St. Louis can help the media develop this awareness.

Notes

[1] Ralph W. Conant, "Black Power: Rhetoric and Reality," *Urban Affairs Quarterly*, September 1968, pp. 15-25.

[2] Jack Lyle (ed.), *Black Americans and the Press* (Los Angeles: Ward Ritchie Press, 1968), pp. xii-xiii.

CHAPTER EIGHT

Prescription for the Press

by WILLIAM L. RIVERS

> The conflict in council sessions is healthy. It forces people to stop and think. Like a toothache, it's a warning.
> —St. Louis press council member

What are the effects of these councils?

Some were described by the authors as they explored their experiences in the foregoing chapter. Others are evident from the quotations of council members and news executives. It may be valuable here, though, to look at the experiments to determine how much can be learned.

First, it is important to point out that the media were not transformed by councils. The newspapers and the radio and television stations remained pretty much what they were. Most of the changes were of degree, not kind—and many were by very few degrees. Anyone who expected a council to turn a small-city daily or weekly into a reasonably exact facsimile of the New York *Times* might say the councils had little effect. But we who conducted the experiments recognize limitations imposed by geography, economics, and myriad other factors. Our goals were more modest, and we came away convinced the councils were a distinct success.

In such circumstances, it may be better to consider other judgments. Donald Brignolo of the University of Missouri reviewed the evidence and concluded that press councils have three important effects:

1. A council tends to lead news executives to a greater awareness of the need for responsible press performance.
2. A council serves a valuable public relations function. It

enables news executives to explain newspaper policy and practice to their audiences and at the same time allows citizens to make their needs known.

3. The presence of a council increases the esteem and understanding of the news media in the eyes of council members and other citizens.[1]

Brignolo's judgments are quite similar to ours, and most of the council members and news executives agree. All the researchers were impressed by the information-seeking of council members, few of whom seemed to have even a rudimentary knowledge of how news media work. Starck reported that although Cairo council members seemed to know what an editorial page was supposed to do, they knew embarrassingly little about newsgathering, production, and management. "When you get right down to it," one member said, "we don't really know much about how a newspaper operates. I don't even know how many reporters [the editor] has. Where does all the news come from? How does the newspaper go about covering local news—for example, education news?"

The Central Questions

Council members not only learned the answers to such questions, in their own way they struck deep at the roots of the work of a free press, as Blankenburg made clear. Consider some of the community-oriented questions raised in the Bend and Redwood City councils:

Does the press transmit its own views and ignore others? At the level of community press councils, the questions is more pointed: Does your Republican editorial page influence your news judgment? Did the *Tribune* headline *How to Keep Unions Away from the Door* attack labor? Does the *Bulletin* scare away correspondents by rebutting letters to the editor?

Is the press influenced by advertisers? The councils asked: Why didn't the *Bulletin* label a ten-page supplement about a new bottling plant as advertising? Why did the *Tribune* allow a chain store to advertise itself as "going out of business" when in fact it was not? Why didn't the paper run more consumer-protection features? Does this photo of an apartment-house development constitute unpaid advertising?

Does the press forsake the significant for the trivial? Why don't you report the community's deep feelings about the schools' proposed modular scheduling system? Why don't you cover trials as fully as arrests? Can't you summarize accident reports to give reporters more time for important stories? Can't you report what it means to Bend workers if two lumber firms merge?

Does the press resist social change? Where do you recruit your staff? Could you hire some black reporters? Why must women have segregated news? Do the people of Bend realize that they have pockets of poverty? Is Redwood City racist? Shouldn't the *Tribune* at least listen to the views of radicals? Shouldn't the media promote social change by exposing racism and providing a more positive image of blacks?

Does the press invade individual privacy? Why publish the names of juvenile offenders? Should their parents' names be listed? Why does the *Bulletin* carry so many stories on plane crash victims? What should the *Tribune* do about the black candidate who doesn't want her picture published?

From this perspective it appears that a press council seldom deals in trivia. One way or another, everything it does—every question it asks—is potentially significant. The publishers generally recognized this, and profited from the frequent reminders of their responsibility.

The Stimulus

A noteworthy result of the Mellett Fund-sponsored councils is that they have stimulated similar efforts. The Denver, Colorado, suburb of Littleton now boasts an active council for two strong weeklies, the Littleton *Independent* and the Arapahoe *Herald,* which are under one ownership. The *Independent*, which won the National Newspaper Association's 1970 National Community Service award and which is owned and edited by Garrett Ray, was formerly edited by Houstoun Waring, an old hand at seeking citizen advice. In 1946, Waring started the Colorado Editorial Advisory Board, bringing several Colorado newspapermen together with specialists in foreign affairs, sociology, economics, political science, and other disciplines. That lasted for six years. Then Waring established an Annual Critics' Dinner to listen to ten leading citizens describe how they would run the Littleton papers. Finally, he set up Sunday morning breakfasts at which he and two other local leaders questioned specialists.

When Waring heard that the Mellett Fund was sponsoring press councils, he and Ray decided to establish one for their papers. They did not invite close friends to serve. As Waring explained, "We see such folks every day. What we wanted was activists, people who lived in various parts of our trade territory, represented both sexes, included the white and black races, and devoted their lives to different programs. We sent out invitations to some people we had never even seen."

The Littleton council included a YMCA director, a youth activities chairman for the Council on Human Relations, a Camp Fire leader, a sociologist, a Boy Scout executive, a high school senior, a political scientist, a Methodist minister, and an oil company scientist who was a member of the Littleton recreation and park board. The scientist was elected council chairman.

Waring and Ray had planned to attend only one in four council meetings so that members could criticize without restraint. But the council asked that at least one representative of the paper attend every meeting to observe and to provide information. "We have no inhibitions about speaking up in front of you," one member told the news executives. That there were no inhibitions was indisputably proved at the first meeting. Members argued that the Littleton papers should use more guest editorials, move obituaries from the front to inside pages, and report more about eminent domain in relation to Denver urban renewal.

Ray and Waring have shared the council's criticisms and suggestions with their readers. In a May 1970 editorial column Ray reported that some council members had attacked and others defended a story exploring rumors that had circulated in Littleton after the death of a young girl. Ray wrote:

> Critical press council members said publishing rumors simply spreads the rumors and makes them more sensational, even if they're recounted in an unsensational way. Our defenders pointed out that we had tried to obtain the truth behind the widely circulated rumors, printing what facts were available as well as the rumors themselves. One Littletonite thought the publications actually helped to reduce the rumors to a less inflammatory level in this case. There was no consensus, and we aren't trying to get one, but the discussion will help us when similar problems arise in the future.[2]

The Mellett Fund experiments also led to the establishment of the Honolulu council, but for reasons quite different from those underlying the Littleton council. In 1969, Honolulu mayor Frank Fasi barred Honolulu *Star-Bulletin* reporters from his office and ordered city department heads not to talk to them because he felt the paper was guilty of unethical reporting in several stories. "I truly hope," Fasi said, "the outcome of this will be an answer to the question: Can a medium throw scruples and ethics out the window and still have the right to cry violation of freedom of the press?"

When both the *Star-Bulletin* and the *Advertiser*, Honolulu's other major paper, deplored the action, mayor Fasi challenged the editors of both papers to a television debate. They declined, saying they did not want to become involved in "theatrics."

The impasse lasted for months, with *Star-Bulletin* reporters covering city hall as best they could without talking with the mayor or his department heads. By January 1970, Dr. Jim Richstad of the University of Hawaii and the Reverend Dr. Claude Du Teil had arranged an elaborate conference at the university to discuss the abrasive relations between the press and the government. Although the struggle between mayor Fasi and the *Star-Bulletin* provided the impetus, an editorial in the *Advertiser* made it clear that there were other reasons:

> The overriding point is that the news media—like everybody else these days—need better communication with the community they serve about the way they serve.
>
> We also feel there is a need for the community to better understand all the news media, for there is a vast body of ignorance and folklore about how news is gathered and presented.
>
> One subject that will be up today is the idea of forming a Hawaii News Media Council, a private body to review matters involving the press, TV and radio—a channel of two-way communication, perhaps something of an ombudsman in matters involving the media.
>
> Its range could include topics from the Mayor's complaints to questions on why some stories aren't covered to informal rules for fairness in an election year to exposure of those who use charges against the press for sheer publicity.
>
> If the press is wrong, it could be expected to take its lumps from public criticism. And if it has a proper point, this also is a means for getting it across.
>
> Such a council won't solve anybody's credibility problem by

itself, but it does seem a worthy step in the direction of more mutual understanding.[3]

Among other things, the day-long conference featured a speech by Bend *Bulletin* editor Robert Chandler, who described the operation of the Bend council and urged that similar councils be established throughout the nation. "The average reader is not the Kansas City milkman with a sixth-grade education any more—the education level of our readers in Bend has doubled in the last twenty years," Chandler said. A council, he pointed out, "lets our readers know they have a friend in court in their disputes with the newspaper and lets our news sources know we have a real degree of interest in the integrity of our reporting and editing."

In May 1970, Honolulu began to form a media council by appointing a six-man committee to decide exactly how the membership should be chosen and how the council should operate. After the first planning committee meeting in May 1970, mayor Fasi lifted the ban on *Star-Bulletin* reporters, citing as the reason that the council would "more or less ride herd" on the news media. Later, he asked three Honolulu television stations for regular air time to report on municipal plans and actions. Two turned him down, but KHON-TV gave him a five-minute weekly program. The *Star-Bulletin* gave the mayor a weekly column—which he has sometimes used to attack the paper. By mid-1971, the Honolulu Community-Media Council was well under way and had pushed through the important resolution on reporting from Vietnam cited in Chapter 1. In Hilo, Hawaii, another council was being established.

The Minnesota Newspaper Association was still setting up its council during the summer of 1971, but it had been decided that the Council would consist of nine laymen and nine representatives of the press and would operate independently of the Association. The chairman of the Council, C. Donald Peterson, an associate judge of the Minnesota Supreme Court, announced:

> The Council has a two-fold purpose, both of which are opposite sides of the same coin. The press carries great power for public good in a free society. The Minnesota Press Council wants to be sure that it remains that way.
>
> To insure that this will be a reality, complaint procedures will

be devised through which the public, or those who have grievances about treatment in the press, can be heard.

The grievance machinery will allow hearing persons, who have
exhausted their prerogatives at the local level, to come before the
Press Council and detail their charges of inaccuracies and unfair-
ness in the reporting of public affairs in separate stories or series
of stories—even in headlines.

The Council also will come to the defense of the press, which
is the other side of the coin, should the facts warrant such
action.[4]

Late in 1971, the Massachusetts Daily Newspaper Survey was
established by Massachusetts dailies to evaluate the work of the state's
forty-six dailies.

In Tulsa, the News Media Committee of the city's Community
Relations Commission operates as a press council. The Committee
chairman is the managing editor of the Tulsa *World*, and the Committee
includes representatives of the Tulsa *Tribune* and the Oklahoma *Eagle*,
a black newspaper, and most of the local radio and television stations.
Earl Reeves, a member of the Community Relations Commission and
the News Media Committee, reports that "this Tulsa council is providing a real opportunity for blacks and newsmen to become acquainted
and to examine together the kinds of problems described in the St.
Louis project."

(In 1971, the American Association of Advertising Agencies set
up a fifty-member National Advertising Review Board to review advertising for fraud and misleading claims. The board will try to assure that
ads are factual and honest.)

Guidelines for Councils

Other cities have established councils, and still others are establishing them. All operate differently. In some cities all media are
involved, in others only a newspaper or broadcasting station. The costs
of council operations range from nothing for most of them to a few
hundred dollars a year for those that hold dinner meetings. Probably
typical is the Littleton council budget of less than $100, which pays for
coffee and cookies, meeting announcements, and an annual dinner
meeting. If there is a consensus as to effective operations, these
guidelines may suggest it:

1. A council is effective with nine to fifteen members. Fewer members do not provide the appropriate range of backgrounds and ideas (unless the members are extraordinary). More make the council unwieldy, although the Honolulu council seems to operate well with thirty-one members.

2. Council members should be community leaders, though not just of the local establishment. A leading banker, lawyer, or doctor are important to a well-rounded council, but the membership should also include intellectual leaders from every field: a housewife who is a discussion leader in club and civic life; a fireman, painter, or plumber who can speak for laboring people; a student who is a recognized discussion leader in his circle.

3. Media representatives should attend meetings but should not be in charge of them. Many successful councils elect their own moderator or invite an outsider—usually a university teacher—to serve as chairman. If the teacher has a working knowledge of journalism, so much the better.

4. Preparing and circulating an agenda for each meeting enables members to research some subjects beforehand—or at least think about them—and allows media representatives to review problems. However, members should be free to discuss subjects not listed on the agenda.

5. To be effective, councils should not meet more frequently than once a month. Some have found that quarterly meetings are sufficient. However, more frequent meetings may be valuable at the beginning, since most members are ignorant of journalistic techniques.

6. A great asset to any council is a media executive who has the will to listen to criticisms and suggestions and the authority to make changes. Good council members can be found in any community, but publishers and station managers enthusiastic about improving their performance and not too sensitive to outside advice may be rare.

7. Meetings can focus either on press performance or on community problems. Because the news media are (or should be) covering community problems, discussing them leads inevitably to discussing press performance.

What Effects?

It is still too early to tell whether the council movement will become a central force in American journalism. But it is clear that councils will exist here and there and that publishers and broadcasters who work with councils will talk about them with their colleagues. Talk about councils, in fact, is broader by many concentric circles than is the actual operation of councils.

This much, however, seems certain: If there are not more cooperative ventures such as councils between the media and the public, citizen's groups will increasingly begin to assess media performance without an invitation. This, in fact, has already happened. In his excellent book *How to Talk Back to Your Television Set*,[5] Nicholas Johnson, a member of the Federal Communications Commission, has spelled out in fascinating detail exactly how changes are being forced in broadcasting. In one case, an individual, John Banzhaf, was a pivotal figure. He complained to the FCC that WCBS-TV in New York ran great quantities of cigarette commercials and that the FCC's "fairness doctrine" requires that a broadcaster present all sides of "controversial issues of public importance." Banzhaf won his case, and as a result broadcasters were forced to make available approximately $100 million worth of free advertising for anti-smoking commercials.

Johnson also tells how the United Church of Christ and blacks in Jackson, Mississippi, opposed the application for license renewal of WLBT-TV, a blatantly racist station. When the FCC refused to accord the petitioners "standing," they went to court and won. When the FCC then admitted the church as an active party but still granted the station its license renewal (commissioners Johnson and Kenneth Cox dissented), the petitioners went back to the court of appeals. This time, in some of the harshest language ever directed at a federal regulatory agency, Judge Warren Burger (now Chief Justice of the U.S. Supreme Court) condemned the Commission's "hostility" and ordered it to accept new applications for the WLBT license. Now, in city after city, broadcasters are being challenged when they attempt to renew their licenses.

Given the increasing pressures, it is difficult to understand why more broadcasters do not eagerly embrace the chance to help establish local councils. Surely one of the strongest arguments for renewing a license every three years would be an indication by a broadcaster that he encouraged and assisted the development of a citizens' group designed to assess his work and that he cooperated in its deliberations.

Publishers, too, are finding that groups of their readers are analyzing newspapers on their own. One of the most vocal conferees in Honolulu was eager to form a council that would shut out newspaper representatives. Jack Butler, editor of the Fort Worth *Star-Telegram,* reported in the *Bulletin* of the American Society of Newspaper Editors that a group in his city investigated his paper quite independently. He wrote:

> They didn't ask us.
> They didn't even tell us.
> They just did it.
> The check on the *Star-Telegram* was run by a committee of the Human Relations Commission, a body created by the Fort Worth City Council to set up communications with minorities.
> First I knew of the fact that the HRC was running a check on our fairness and objectivity in news about Negroes: when a young city editor—concerned about an understanding we have that people don't pay a dime for the *Star-Telegram* to read about the editor—called me about the story on the survey results.
> What was bothering him was a statement of the investigating committee that the editor of the *Star-Telegram* "has fully recognized that 'journalism is a priestly mission.'" The reason the committee said that was that the *Star-Telegram* had gotten a completely clean bill of health.
> We suspended the rule that night and carried the story in full and with rejoicing. Although we didn't know we were under the glass, the report described a situation we had worked hard to achieve—and for a long time . . . .
> I have always been against this press council idea—probably being as suspicious of the motives and intellectual honesty of the prospective council as many of our readers are of us. But this report forces me to some second thoughts.
> (Whether this would have been true if it had been unfavorable is another question I decline to debate.)[6]

For many critics, local councils are hardly strong enough to transform the media to the extent that they consider necessary. They are aware that American newspapers and broadcasting stations are local and that their failings are most obvious to local audiences. But the national (and international) reach of the American press associations, syndicates, and broadcasting networks—which provide most of the national and world news that is printed and broadcast through local newspapers and stations—and the increasing numbers of mergers and take-overs that sometimes seem destined to weld the media into a few vast conglomerates—these forces argue for a council with a much stronger sweep and a much wider scope.

The British Press Council

One model for a national council for the United States is the British Press Council, which is designed to improve the performance of British newspapers. Great Britain has many fewer dailies than does the United States, and some of the British papers are national rather than local because they can reach the major population centers rapidly. If for these reasons the British council is not a perfect model for the United States, it still can teach us important lessons.

The British council was born as the result of a threat which surfaced in 1946 when the House of Commons voted to appoint a Royal Commission to investigate the finances, control, management, and ownership of the press in order "to further the free expression of opinion through the press and the greatest practicable accuracy in the presentation of news." Significantly, the motion was moved and seconded by two *journalist* members of Commons who feared that the growth of chains and the advent of big business into newspapers was inhibiting freedom of the press.

Journalism, the Commission decided, was a profession grafted to an industry, having to reconcile the claims of society with the claims of commerce. The Commission recommended establishing a General Council of the Press to maintain standards of professional responsibility and integrity.

Various British press organizations discussed the council idea, and approved it in general, but as H. Phillip Levy notes in *The Press Council,* "The truth is that there was no real enthusiasm in press circles for a press council."[7] In November 1952 a bill was introduced in Commons to legislate the press council into existence. This pushed the press into action, and by February 1953 a joint committee of press organizations had agreed on a draft constitution. Although the Royal Commission had recommended that laymen be included, the council was made up entirely of twenty-five journalists—ten from management, fifteen from editorial staffs.

The complaints that came in to the Commission the first year covered a wide spectrum. Some correspondents were certain that if the newspapers had been open to their ideas for universal peace, the two world wars never would have occurred; others urged the Council to investigate incidents that were decades old.

But many complaints were more immediate and worth investigating. A noted critic, for instance, complained that he had been invited by *The Daily Sketch* to write a series of reviews, but the first one had been twisted by the editors to give another view, though the critic's by-line had remained on the article. The Press Council censured the *Sketch*—and it and other papers printed the Council's statement.

Others complained about the extravagant attention the newspapers gave to the Kinsey Report, and Council issued a widely publicized statement holding that

> . . .this Council, while defending the right of the Press in the contemporary world to deal in an adult manner with matters of sex, is deeply concerned by the unwholesome exploitation of sex by certain newspapers and periodicals. It places on record its view that such treatment is calculated to injure public morals especially because newspapers and periodicals are seen and read by young persons. It is also contrary to those standards of journalism which it is the Council's duty to maintain. The Council intends to keep this matter under review.[8]

The British Press Council continued on this line for several years, praising journalism for such actions as the publicity given to studies showing a relationship between tobacco and lung cancer, attacking it for individual and collective violations of good taste. In the early history, the most frequent complaints received by the Council were for (1) invasion of privacy; (2) violations of good taste; and (3) emphasis on sex.

After nearly ten years of Press Council activity, another Royal Commission was appointed to investigate the deaths of newspapers and growing monopoly characteristic in the industry. The new Commission found increasing concentration. It also reported that the voluntary Press Council's inactivity in the economic field made the case for a statutory body quite clear. The need for lay membership on the Council, the Commission Report stated, was equally clear.

In 1963, the Press Council reconstituted itself, reducing by five the number of professional members and taking in five lay members, including a lay chairman, the famous Lord Devlin. The Council now works this way: a General Purposes Committee deals with positive aspects (protecting freedom of the press by reviewing censorship laws and economic concentration, etc.); a Complaints Committee reviews complaints regarding press performance.

Any citizen may complain, but the Press Council deals with complaints against newspapers, not against individual journalists. Many complaints are rejected because the aggrieved person has not first sought redress from the editor of the paper. The Council also will not consider a complaint if legal action is filed or threatened, until proceedings have been concluded or abandoned.

An aggrieved person who fails to receive satisfaction from an editor must state his complaint in a letter to the Council and must enclose copies of his correspondence with the editor and a copy of the newspaper of the relevant page. He is asked also to give the names and addresses of any witnesses.

The Council then informs the editor and invites his response. Then the Complaint Committee investigates, usually making its conclusions from written statements. On occasion, however, the parties concerned are asked to appear before the Council.

A complete dossier is then prepared for each member of the Council and sent to him before the next meeting. Only the Council members attend the decision. On a few occasions the Council has reversed the recommendations of the Complaints Committee.

Finally, the Council releases a summary of the facts and its decision. Although the editor is held responsible for anything appearing in his paper, individual journalists are sometimes blamed as well. The Council issues two kinds of judgments when it finds a newspaper at fault: admonition or, in serious cases, censure. In one three-year period, there were only two recorded cases in which offending newspapers had failed to publish Council statements critical of their conduct.

The aims of the Press Council as stated in its current constitution are:

(1) To preserve the established freedom of the British Press.

(2) To maintain the character of the British Press in accordance with the highest professional and commercial standards.

(3) To consider complaints about the conduct of the Press or the conduct of persons and organizations towards the Press; to

deal with these complaints in whatever manner might seem practical and appropriate and record resultant action.

(4) To keep under review developments likely to restrict the supply of information of public interest and importance.

(5) To report publicly on developments that may tend toward greater concentration or monopoly in the Press (including changes in ownership, control and growth of Press undertakings) and to publish statistical information relating to them.

(6) To make representations on appropriate occasions to the Government, organs of the United Nations and to Press organizations abroad.

(7) To publish periodical reports recording the Council's work and to review from time to time developments in the Press and the factors affecting them.[9]

Professor Donald E. Brown of Arizona State University reported in 1971 that the scoffing, disdain, and contempt that were so common among editors during the early years of the Press Council have almost disappeared. "Antipathy has been replaced by respect and by a realization that the Council's accomplishments have considerably outweighed its shortcomings," Brown wrote. A prime example is Hugh Cudlipp, who was long the editor of the *Daily Mirror*, the splashy tabloid that has the largest circulation in Britain. Cudlipp wrote a book in 1962 that carried eight references to the Council, all critical. Now the chairman of the International Publishing Corporation, Cudlipp asserts that he and his huge company are "totally in favor of the Press Council." The hard-hitting *Daily Express* snapped in an editorial in 1949, "The proposal for a Press Council is the futile outcome of a phony agitation." But after the Council had been operating for several years, the *Express* held: "It is proper that the watchdogs should themselves have watchdogs."[10]

Citing a study that showed that by 1967 86 percent of the British editors were favorable, Brown wrote that his observations and interviews indicated that the percentage has increased. In fact, the major flaw most editors see in the British Press Council is that it does not assess the performance of radio and television as well as newspapers.[11] (Late in 1971, the British Broadcasting Corporation (BBC) set up a commission to review complaints from those who thought they were unfairly treated on radio or television. The commission is made up of three laymen who decide their own procedures. The BBC will publish the commission's adjudications.)

The British journalists' applause is not the result of their being treated favorably by the Council. Of the 446 complaints adjudicated during the past six years, the council upheld the readers and criticized the newspapers in 247 cases.[12] Although the Council has no legal power, it has succeeded because it has used wisely a weapon the press has learned to respect: publicity.

A National Council Here?

Several plans for a national council in the United States are even more comprehensive than the British Press Council. One, issued in 1947 by the privately financed Commission on Freedom of the Press, recommended an agency to appraise and report annually on media performance. The agency was to be independent of government and of the press, created by gifts, and it was to be given a ten-year trial. Its work would include:

1. Continuing efforts, through conferences with practitioners and analysis by its staff, to help the press define workable standards of performance . . . .

2. Pointing out the inadequacy of press service in certain areas and the trend toward concentration in others, to the end that local communities and the press itself may organize to supply service where it is lacking or to provide alternative service where the drift toward monopoly seems dangerous.

3. Inquiries in areas where minority groups are excluded from reasonable access to the channels of communication.

4. Inquiries abroad regarding the picture of American life presented by the American press; and cooperation with agencies in other countries and with international agencies engaged in analysis of communication across national borders.

5. Investigation of instances of press lying, with particular reference to persistent misrepresentation of the data required for judging public issues.

6. Periodic appraisal of the tendencies and characteristics of the various branches of the communications industry.

7. Continuous appraisal of governmental action affecting communications.

8. Encouragement of the establishment of centers of advanced study, research, and criticism in the field of communications at universities.

9. Encouragement of projects which give hope of meeting the needs of special audiences.

10. The widest possible publicity and public discussion on all the foregoing.[13]

The Commission on Freedom of the Press argued that such an agency would both hold the press accountable and enable it to remain free. Thus, press performance would be brought much closer to what the commission declared were the five ideal demands of society for communicating news and ideas:

(1) a truthful, comprehensive, and intelligent account of the day's events in a context which gives them meaning; (2) a forum for the exchange of comment and criticism; (3) the projection of a representative picture of the constituent groups in the society; (4) the presentation and clarification of the goals and values of the society; (5) full access to the day's intelligence."[14]

Nothing was done to implement this plan, and for years it was little discussed except in universities. But recently, because of a rising tide of displeasure with the media, individuals and agencies have built upon the Commission's suggestions and have produced a startling variety of programs for assessing media performance. Perhaps the most comprehensive—and expensive—was issued in 1969 by a task force of the National Commission on the Causes and Prevention of Violence. In a closely argued section of its volume on *Violence and the Media,* the members of the task force suggested the establishment of a Center for Media Study which would be "independently administered, maintained, and financed, and should have the requisite national standing and absolutely essential independence to insure that its findings and judgments would be subject to minimum influence by the media or government."

The task force recommended, however, that the President of the United States set the agency in motion:

To assure the political as well as the economic independence of the Center, the President should select a Governing Board of prominent non-political and non-media public figures, with significant social and economic minority representation. To insure that the Center has access to the specialized knowledge and competence available in the media, the President should also select a Media Advisory Board from nominees submitted directly by the media themselves. Finally, the President should appoint a Research Board from among distinguished specialists in such diverse but relevant disciplines as communications research, social psychology, sociology, cultural anthropology, communications technology, law, psychiatry, economics, and management. . . .

If the media are to be responsible directly to the people, as Dr. [Frank] Stanton of CBS and others have suggested, we believe it appropriate for the people to be asked to participate directly in a proposal to examine how well the media discharge that responsibility. We suggest that individual contributions be solicited through a nationwide advertising campaign, planned as a public service by the Advertising Council, and carried as public service advertising in all of the mass media. Supplemental advertising space or time could be purchased either from funds provided initially by a foundation or from contributions received from the public. As an incentive for individual contributions, there would be the usual Federal income tax deduction. A more viable alternative, however, would be a direct Federal tax credit of up to five dollars per person. If contributions exceed the amounts needed to operate the Center, the excess funds could be invested in government securities, with a set percentage of the proceeds used, for example, to endow additional scholarships, to supplement mid-career training programs, or to be added to the Center's endowment.

Supplemental means of financing would include a dedicated tax on advertising or the sale of radio and television receivers, on gross receipts of the media, or on foundations. One disadvantage of the dedicated tax is that the money passes through government control. The objection could be partially met by placing the funds in a trust account, free from the annual appropriations process.[15]

The task force recommendations have not been implemented,

perhaps because, despite the efforts to make the prospective agency an independent body, the taint—or at least the touch—of government is clear upon the structure.

Others who have proposed a critical agency include Professor Harold Lasswell of Yale, who was a member of the Commission on Freedom of the Press of the 1940s. He has suggested a private, nonprofit Commission on Public Communications which would be governed by (1) a policy board to "take responsibility for the statement of the criteria to be applied in appraising the media, and for periodic interpretations of available research data" and (2) a research board to be "responsible for translating statements of goals or objectives in research terms." Recognizing that a link to government would doom the proposal, Lasswell hoped that the commission he suggested would be sponsored by a private foundation or a major university, with funding by foundations, the communications industry itself, or by other businesses.

What is clear from these and other proposals—at least a dozen were being promoted as the 1970s began—is that many individuals and organizations are deadly serious in their efforts to push the media toward more responsible performance. All of the responsible proposals are for agencies that would publicize rather than apply sanctions. And yet the fervor of many of the proponents of a national council should be a warning to journalists.

Editor & Publisher, the trade weekly of the newspaper industry, recently carried an editorial that frowned on a national press council because few editors "want to play judge, jury and prosecutor over the performances of their peers mainly because that's what freedom of the press is all about."[16] That is not, of course, what freedom of the press is all about. It is about a free society's effort to promote free expression, and journalists who are so eager to judge the other institutions of society must not hesitate to join in judging their own kind, for few institutions are as powerful or as in need of judgment—and pitiless publicity—as the mass media.

Let journalists consider the consequences of refusing to cooperate with the inevitable—the consequences of standing by while the public asserts itself. The great danger is that the people may begin to measure their access to the media against the First Amendment guarantee. This could lead to the discovery of a singular fact: The First Amendment was quite different when this country was founded because almost any literate man could take advantage of press freedom. Today, however, freedom of the press is the only guarantee in the Bill of Rights that cannot be exercised effectively by individuals. Discoveries lead to changes, and there is nothing in the Constitution that prohibits amending an amendment. If responsible publishers and broadcasters believe, as I do, that tinkering with the First Amendment is dangerous, they will not oppose a national press council but promote it.

Notes

[1] Donald E. Brignolo, "Community Press Councils," Freedom of Information Center Report No. 217, University of Missouri, March 1969.

[2] Garrett Ray, "Scratch Pad," Littleton *Independent* May 26, 1970, p. 8.

[3] "Our Credibility Gap," Honolulu *Advertiser*, January 13, 1970, p. 14.

[4] Gerald B. Healey, "Press Council in Minnesota Hailed for Two-Way Education," *Editor & Publisher*, April 3, 1971, p. 12.

[5] Nicholas Johnson, *How to Talk Back to Your Television Set* (Boston: Little, Brown, 1970), pp. 203-205.

[6] Jack Butler, "Minority Coverage Under the Glass," *The Bulletin of the American Society of Newspaper Editors*, March 1969, p. 4.

[7] H. Phillip Levy, *The Press Council* (New York: St. Martin's Press, 1967), p. 9.

[8] *Ibid.*, pp. 321-22.

[9] *Ibid.*, pp. 19-20.

[10] Donald E. Brown, "British Journalists Change Their Attitudes Toward Reorganized Press Council," *Editor & Publisher*, April 17, 1971, p. 22.

[11] *Ibid.*, p. 22.

[12] Donald E. Brown, "Press Council Rulings Serve as Guidelines for Journalists," *Editor & Publisher*, April 24, 1971, p. 17.

[13] Commission on Freedom of the Press, *A Free and Responsible Press* (Chicago: University of Chicago Press, 1947), pp. 101-102.

[14] *Ibid.*, pp. 21-29.

[15] David L. Lange *et al.*, *Mass Media and Violence*, Vol. 9 of *A Report to the National Commission on the Causes and Prevention of Violence* (Washington, D.C.: U.S. Government Printing Office, 1969), pp. 287-88.

[16] "What About Press Councils?", *Editor & Publisher*, November 28, 1970, p. 4.

A Press Council Bibliography

Note: The asterisk denotes those references devoted entirely to the press council.

Books

Associated Press Managing Editors Association, *The APME Red Book 1969*, Vol. XXII. New York: The Associated Press, 1969.

Baker, Robert K., and Sandra I. Ball, eds., *Violence and the Media: A Report to the National Commission on the Causes and Prevention of Violence*, Vol. 9. Washington, D.C.: U.S. Government Printing Office, 1969, pp. 381-93.

*Bingham, Barry, "Why Not Local Press Councils?", in *Press Councils and Press Codes*, 3rd ed. Zurich: The International Press Institute, November 1964, pp. 68-70.

Breed, Walter, "Social Control in the News Room: A Functional Analysis," in Wilbur Schramm, ed., *Mass Communications*, 2nd. ed. Urbana, Ill.: University of Illinois Press, 1960, pp. 178-94.

Casey, Ralph, ed., *The Press in Perspective*. Baton Rouge, La.: Louisiana State University Press, 1963.

Commission on Freedom of the Press, *A Free and Responsible Press*. Chicago: University of Chicago Press, 1947.

Gerald, J. Edward, *The Social Responsibility of the Press*. Minneapolis, Minn.: University of Minnesota Press, 1963.

Hohenberg, John, *Free Press/Free People: The Best Cause*. New York: Columbia University Press, 1971.

*Levy, H. Phillip, *The Press Council: History, Procedure and Cases*. New York: St. Martin's Press, 1967.

*Murray, George, The *Press and the Public: The Story of the British Press Council*. Carbondale, Ill.: Southern Illinois University Press, 1972.

National Advisory Commission on Civil Disorders (Kerner Commission), *Report of the National Advisory Commission on Civil Disorders.* New York: Bantam Books, 1968, pp. 362-89.

Reston, James, *The Artillery of the Press.* New York: Harper & Row, 1966.

Rivers, William L., and Wilbur Schramm, *Responsibility in Mass Communications,* rev. ed., New York: Harper & Row, 1969.

Periodicals

*"Advisory Council," *Editor & Publisher,* July 28, 1951, p. 36.

*Arnold, Edmund C., "The Ombudsman's Children . . . Do They Need a Press Council?", *The Quill,* September 1968, pp. 14-16.

*Bagdikian, Ben H., "The Awakening of the U.S. Press to Changing Societies," *IPI Report,* December 1969, pp. 11-12.

Barron, Jerome, "Access to the Press—A New First Amendment Right," *Harvard Law Review,* 1967, pp. 1641-78.

*Blankenburg, William B., "Local Press Councils: An Informal Accounting," *Columbia Journalism Review,* Spring 1969, pp. 14-17.

*Brignolo, Donald E., "Community Press Councils," *Freedom of Information Center Report No. 217,* University of Missouri School of Journalism, March 1969, and reprinted in *Seminar,* December 1969, pp. 13-18.

*Brown, Donald E., "British Journalists Change Their Attitudes Toward Reorganized Press Council," *Editor & Publisher,* April 17, 1971, pp. 22, 58, 60, 62.

*———, "Press Council Rulings Serve as Guidelines for Journalists," *Editor & Publisher,* April 24, 1971, pp. 17, 22, 24, 30, 34.

*Chandler, Bob, "Editor's Bane or Salvation?", *The Bulletin of the American Society of Newspaper Editors,* May 1969, pp. 7-8.

Donohew, Lewis, "Publishers and Their 'Influence' Groups," *Journalism Quarterly,* Winter 1965, pp. 112-13.

Erskine, Hazel, "The Polls: Opinion of the News Media," *Public Opinion Quarterly,* Winter 1970-71, pp. 630-43.

Even-Zohar, Chaim, "Fresno Survey Shows Distorted View of Newspaper's Function," *Publishers' Auxiliary,* May 15, 1971, p. 24.

*Healey, Gerald B., "Press Council in Minnesota Hailed for Two-Way Education," *Editor & Publisher,* April 3, 1971, p. 12.

Huston, Luther, "Noyes Urges ASNE Members to Guard Their Perspective," *Editor & Publisher,* April 17, 1971, p. 15.

*Isaacs, Norman E., "Why We Lack a National Press Council," *Columbia Journalism Review,* Fall 1970, pp. 16-26.

*Markham, James W., *et al.,* "Journalism Educators and the Press Council Idea: A Symposium," *Journalism Quarterly,* Spring 1968, pp. 77-85.

*"Press Councils—Well, Ye . . . es, but in What Form?", *IPI Report,* June/July 1970, pp. 9-11.

*Schneider, Lawrence, "A Media-Black Council: Seattle's 19-Month Experiment," *Journalism Quarterly,* Autumn 1970, pp. 439-49.

*Starck, Kenneth, "What Community Press Councils Talk About," *Journalism Quarterly,* Spring 1970, pp. 20-26.

*———, "Community Press Councils in Southern Illinois," *Grassroots Editor,* November-December 1968, pp. 3-7.

*———, "Concerning Press Councils . . . Anatomy of a Press Council," *Grassroots Editor,* May-June 1970, pp. 18-22.

*Tobin, Richard L., "Does the U.S. Need a National Press Council?", *Saturday Review,* October 14, 1967, pp. 115-16.

Unpublished Material

*Atwood, L. Erwin, and Kenneth Starck, "Evaluating the Community Press Council." Paper presented at annual convention of the Association for Education in Journalism, American University, Washington, D.C., August 1970.

*Blankenburg, William B., "Community Press Councils." Doctoral dissertation, Stanford University, August 1968.

*Chandler, Robert W., "Information About the Bend, Ore., Press Council" (mimeographed), January 1970.

*Long, Howard R., and Kenneth Starck, "Pilot Demonstration on Developing Community Press Councils in Southern Illinois." Report prepared for the Mellett Fund for a Free and Responsible Press, October 1968.

*Reeves, Earl J., "Report on the Community Communications Council for St. Louis." Report prepared for the Mellett Fund for a Free and Responsible Press, March 1969.

*Snider, Paul B., "The British Press Council: A Study of Its Role and Performance, 1953-1965." Doctoral dissertation, University of Iowa, 1968.

*Starck, Kenneth, "Press Regulation of Itself." Paper presented at 85th annual National Newspaper Association convention, June 26, 1970, Des Moines, Iowa.

*———, "Press Listening Post: American Newspapers Respond to the Council Concept." Paper presented at Southern Newspaper Publishers Association Foundation Seminar, August 15-18, 1971, Oklahoma State University.

Minnesota Press Council Grievance Committee Procedural Rules

One of the primary functions of the Minnesota Press Council is consideration and processing of grievances against the Press and the editors and employees of the Press. The Council will undertake to hear, consider and adjust grievances after determining the essential facts of any controversy through hearings and any necessary investigations. In order to function effectively and fairly it is essential that a separate Grievance Committee be created and that operating procedures be established for the Committee. While a complete set of procedural rules must be provided for those instances where proper consideration of the grievance will require application of a full range of procedural rules, it is expected that the vast majority of grievances will not require such formal handling. For example, while due process rights such as the right of counsel is provided, it is expected that the parties will seek to have their attorneys directly involved only on very rare occasions in the processing of a grievance. The nature of the Council's function is such that informality of the proceedings is beneficial and formality at every stage will be discouraged.

While the composition of the Grievance Committee is not properly a subject for inclusion in these procedural rules, these rules are based upon the expectation that the Grievance Committee will be structured to directly reflect the same composition of public and professional interests as are reflected in the membership of the Press Council.

As used in these procedural rules the following terms shall be considered technical terms and to have the following meaning:

Press: Newspapers of general circulation in the state of Minnesota

Newspaper: The particular newspaper against whom a complaint or grievance has been made

Complainant: A person or organization who has or makes a grievance against a newspaper

I.   Instituting or Commencing Grievances

A. *Exhaustion of local remedies. No grievance should be processed unless the matter has first been presented to the newspaper by the complainant.*

Comment

The purpose of the Press Council is primarily to encourage mutual understanding between the Press and the local citizenry. One of the simplest and most effective methods to insure mutual understanding is personal face to face discussion of problem areas and disputes among the persons involved. The discussion should involve the editor or publisher of the newspaper and the complainant directly. By this personal meeting imagined affronts and misunderstandings can often be cleared up. If personal discussion with the local editor is made first, it will give the editor an opportunity to understand the nature and extent of the complainant's concern, to be advised more clearly regarding matters that are occurring in his community, and to more precisely present the newspaper's position. If the newspaper agrees it is in error, it will be possible for immediate corrective action to be taken by the newspaper, including publishing corrections. If the matter is not an error of the newspaper, but arises through misunderstanding by the complainant of the function of the Press, perhaps discussion of professional standards and understanding of the problems of the Press will resolve the problem at that point. If nothing else, at least the parties will be introduced to each other and the areas of dispute acknowledged and recognized between them.

Each grievance shall be temporarily withheld from further processing until the grievance has been presented to the newspaper and the newspaper has been given an opportunity to discuss the matter with the complainant and for such time as may be reasonably necessary for the parties to take such corrective actions as either party may deem desirable.

B. *Grievances can be brought by individuals and private and public entities against a newspaper, but not against individual employees of the newspaper.*

Comment

The newspaper should be considered responsible for the conduct of all of its employees in terms of the newspaper's relationship to the public. Therefore the grievance should be directed against the newspaper even though the actual cause may arise from conduct by a individual editor, reporter, or other employee.

In those grievances where it appears that a reporter's or other employee's professional conduct is the primary source of the grievance, the reporter or employee involved should be personally informed of the grievance and given an opportunity to participate directly in the proceeding as though he were in fact a party to the proceeding. In no event, however, will the newspaper be relieved of its ultimate responsibility for the conduct of its employees or be permitted to have the grievance dropped as to it. At all times it must be recognized that it is the complainant's grievance that is the sole issue before the Grievance Committee.

C. *No grievance will be considered if legal action based on the same subject matter is pending against the newspaper or an individual journalist. A grievance will not be processed until the complainant waives any possible future civil action that he may have arising out of the grievance for matters occurring prior to the filing of the grievance.*

Comment

It would seem desirable for the Council not to be involved in grievances in which litigation is pending. In like measure, it would not be desirable for the Council to consider a matter when the same or related matter may ultimately be presented to a court as a part of a civil claim. If a complainant wishes to invoke the process of the Press Council, he should recognize his resort to the Press Council will be his exclusive remedy for all matters relating to the subject matter of the grievance. Waiver of civil actions, of course, should not be waivers of legal actions for future incidents of alleged misconduct or repetition of the matter involved in the pending complaint.

D. *A party filing a grievance should waive libel and slander claims against persons providing the council with information, against members of the Council and against the Press for publication of information acquired by the Council during its investigation and hearing process, or included in the Council's report.*

Comment

Proceedings by the Press Council are not protected by statutory privilege. As such, the Council should undertake to provide protection to persons giving information to the Press Council and protection to members of the Council to encourage high level professional and citizen involvement in the Council activities. Waiver of libel and slander claims contribute some incentive for full and complete participation both by the public, Council members, and the Press.

E. *Grievances resolved by agreement between the complainant and the newspaper following its presentation to the newspaper should not be further processed and the matter should be dropped at that point. No formal record should be kept of the grievance thus resolved.*

Comment

If the matter is disposed of following the initial presentation of the grievance to the newspaper, it would seem that the adjustment is personal and between the parties. The Press Council should not review the adjustment or indicate any assent or dissent to the arrangement. Since no responsibility is taken for the action, a record should not be maintained for the details of the initial inquiry other than the fact that it has been disposed of by personal adjustment.

F. *Grievances to be further considered by the Council must be filed with the council in written form.*

Comment

If the complainant has difficulty expressing his grievance to written form, members of the Council staff should be free to assist the complainant in this endeavor. Care should be taken by the staff to insure that the facts are accurately expressed and that the staff person does not improperly influence or suggest additional areas of concern to the complainant.

II. Grievance Processing

A. *Upon receipt of a written grievance, a copy of the grievance must be sent to the newspaper with a request that the newspaper reply promptly to the grievance in writing setting forth the newspaper's contentions.*

Comment

Procedurally it is desirable that each party's formal position be reflected by written statements. Since a written grievance initiates the process, it would seem desirable to have the newspaper's response also in written form. By compelling a writing at an early stage, the parties are less free to change positions factually later on in the proceedings, but more importantly, the parties are forced to think through their positions more clearly. There is no prejudice to the newspaper if the newspaper refuses to cooperate with the Council at this stage and refuses to provide a written statement. The opportunity to make a statement is a privilege, not an obligation. A failure to respond does not indicate agreement with the facts asserted in the grievance. A right to participate personally in future hearings can be denied until a written response is made.

B. *The Grievance Committee will review each filed grievance. The Committee may establish and adopt a procedure for processing grievances, including a method for a preliminary screening of grievances.*

Comment

The Grievance Committee should be responsible for determining the sufficiency of each filed grievance and for adopting its own policies with regard to the method of processing grievances best designed to insure proper processing. The Committee should be free to adopt a preliminary screening procedure if it desires. In like measure, the Committee should have the freedom to determine whether or not each grievance must be processed by the entire Committee as a preliminary matter. Once the Committee has experience in processing grievances, the Committee should be free to amend its internal procedures without the necessity of obtaining approval from the entire Press Council and requiring an amendment to these procedural rules.

C. *The Grievance Committee shall make a preliminary and informal fact investigation including discussions with the complainant, the newspaper, the newspaper's reporters or employees, and witnesses. The investigation may be conducted by a designated staff person or members of the Committee and can involve written communication as well as personal conferences or telephone communication.*

Comment

Preliminary informal fact investigation is desirable to verify the facts alleged in the grievance and in the response. The Committee should be free to adopt whatever method is most desirable in a particular case or type of case for determining accuracy of statements and resolving questions regarding the nature of the grievance. No formal investigation steps should be required other than those steps the Committee deems necessary to determine whether or not a grievance is factually meritorious.

D. *If the grievance should be dismissed after preliminary investigation, the Grievance Committee should so advise the Press Council and if concurred in by the Press Council, copies of the dismissal will be transmitted in written form to the complainant and to the newspaper together with a brief statement explaining the reasons for the dismissal.*

E. *A record will be kept of all grievances and the disposition of the grievance, including letters of dismissals. A summary of the record will be sent to all Council members periodically for their information.*

F. *If the Grievance Committee decides further Committee action is necessary, a hearing time will be scheduled for the Committee to consider the evidence and hear witnesses presented by the parties. All parties will have the opportunity to appear in person before the Committee and give oral testimony. Non-party witnesses can be called and examined only in the discretion of the Committee. A right to cross examination and a right to counsel are available for both parties. Normally no transcript of the hearing will be made, but the Committee or any party shall have the privilege of preserving the evidence in any reasonable manner he chooses, such as the use of tape recordings, etc. At all times the desirability of informality and flexibility of the proceedings must be recognized.*

Comment

A hearing may be necesssry for the Committee to get a true flavor of the dispute and to determine the credibility of persons giving evidence by observing their demeanor. Basic due process requirements of confrontation, cross-examination and counsel should be available if the parties desire to exercise those rights, but such use should be discouraged and should be the exception, not the rule. The British believe that this type of administrative proceedings should not involve due process procedural protection. In this country it is generally believed that better factual results will be obtained if due process requirements are available for those rare situations where they are needed, or for persons who would feel more comfortable if assisted by an attorney, or for persons who want to examine an adverse witness.

G. *Additional investigations can be made and additional evidence can be presented to the Committee after the hearing at the direction of the Committee.*

Comment

At the end of the hearing questions may still exist with regard to fact matters. The Committee should be able to obtain this information either by investigation or by additional hearings.

H. *The Grievance Committee by majority vote will make the Committee's decision on the matter and recommend corrective action if any is deemed desirable. If a grievance involves a matter of broad general policy or could involve more than the one newspaper grieved against, the grievance must be transmitted to the Press Council for deliberation with or without recommendation by the Grievance Committee.*

Comment

Certain grievances may involve matters of general policy that properly should be considered as policy questions by the entire Press Council. Such grievances must be considered and resolved by the Council, and the Grievance Committee is free to refer such a grievance to the Press

Council at any stage of its proceeding whenever the Committee feels that such referral is proper.

III. Recommendations and Reports

A. *Except for grievances involving matters of general policy covered under II, H, conclusions and recommendations of the Grievance Committee will be transmitted to each of the parties in writing. Each party will be given a period of ten days to submit responses to the recommendations in writing before consideration of the recommendations by the Press Council.*

Comment

It would seem desirable that each party be advised of the intended report before public release of the recommendations of the Grievance Committee. If errors are made factually or legally the parties will have an opportunity to correct such errors.

B. *All recommendations of the Grievance Committee will be transmitted to the Press Council for its consideration.*

Comment

The recommendation of the Grievance Committee and the parties' response thereto should be sent to all members of the Press Council prior to the Council meeting.

C. *The Press Council will consider the recommendation of the Grievance Committee, and by majority of the Press Council members voting on the question can accept, reject, or amend the recommendation, or it can return the grievance to the Committee for further processing. After final action by the Press Council, the Press Council will make a written report of its action.*

D. *The report of the Press Council will be transmitted to the parties and to the news media for publication.*

IV. Appeal to the Council

A. *Appeals from a dismissal by the Grievance Committee, or from a report of the Council in grievances where the parties have not previously appeared before the Council, will be permitted only at the discretion of the Press Council.*

Comment

An automatic appeal with an extended hearing by the entire Council in each case would not be beneficial in terms of preserving Grievance Committee integrity or in permitting the Council time to consider its other functions. Appeals involving new fact hearings should be the exception, not the rule. No party has a right to a new fact hearing or to appear personally before the entire Council. Such matters should be discretionary with the Press Council.

B. *Such appeals to the Press Council, when granted, ordinarily shall not be hearings de novo, but in the discretion of the Council new evidence may be heard.*

C. *The Press Council's deliberations need not be public.*

D. *Following the Press Council's deliberations, its recommendations will be reported to each of the parties and to the Press in the form of a report and the report can be published.*